Life out of death
The feminine spirit in El Salvador

Life out of death
The feminine spirit in El Salvador

Women in conversation with
Marigold Best and Pamela Hussey

With a theological reflection by
Marcella Althaus-Reid

First published 1996
Catholic Institute for International Relations
Unit 3, Canonbury Yard, 190a New North Road,
London N1 7BJ, UK.

Life out of Death: The feminine spirit in El Salvador
© CIIR 1996

British Library Cataloguing in Publication Data
A catalogue record for this book is available from the
British Library

ISBN 1852 87 189 X

Cover photo: Trainee catechists in Gotera, El Salvador, 1989.
Steve Smith/Andes Press Agency.

Design by Rich Cowley
Printed by Hobbs the Printers, Totton, UK.

Contents

Introduction   1

El Salvador: Historical background   11

Archbishops of San Salvador   15

The women:

Carmen Manuela del Cid   20

A new way of being church: San Antonio Abad   30

Sisters of St Clare, San Antonio Abad   40

The novices: Sisters of St Clare, San Antonio Abad   47

Sister Mark: Sisters of St Clare, Gotera, Morazán   50

A new way of being a sister: The Little Community   55

A new way of praying: A 'pray-in' at San Antonio Abad   62

Women learning to stand on their own:
     The archdiocesan women's programme   65

Rufina Amaya: Ciudad Segundo Montes   72

Sandra, in Perquín:
     The subversive memory of the people   79

Andrea, women's group coordinator, Nueva Esperanza   85

María Julia Hernández:
     Director of the archdiocesan legal aid office   94

Sisters Patricia Farrell and Peggy O'Neill:
     North Americans working in Suchitoto   96

The women of Suchitoto   104

The story of Doña Isabel, Guarjila, Chalatenango   120

Conversation with Suyapa: Guarjila, Chalatenango   127

The Salvadorean Women's Movement   137

Dolores: A valiant woman   139

Isabel Ascencio   142

Mercedes Cañas: Centre for Feminist Studies   153

Morena Herrera: Women for Dignity and Life   166

Ana Gloria and Mónica   176

Silvia   184

Ana Guadalupe Martínez:
   From student to FMLN militant to
   vice-president of the Legislative Assembly   188

A reflection by Marcella Althaus-Reid

Doing the theology of memory:
   Counting crosses and resurrections   194

Bibliography   207

About the authors   210

Glossary

Arpilleristas	women weavers
Barrio	neighbourhood
Base ecclesial communities/ base Christian communities	small groups of people, mostly poor, who meet to reflect on the Bible and on their life situation. There are many of these groups in Latin America, with different origins and history in each country. Central American BECs have a deep experience of martyrdom.
Base organisation	grassroots organisation
Canton	ward, subdivision of a municipality
Capture	a term often used rather than 'arrest' to describe people being picked up and taken away without proper authority, even if by the police. 'Arrest' would denote a legal action.
Catechists/ catechetics teacher	lay woman or man, usually trained by a sister or priest
Celebrants of the word	woman or man trained to comment on the Bible and to carry out other pastoral work in the base ecclesial communities. Where a priest is not available for the eucharist, a celebrant of the word will organise readings from the Bible followed by commentaries by the people drawing on their own experiences.
Colón	El Salvadorean currency (8 *colones* = 1US$, 1994)
Comandante	military commander/leader/officer
Community teacher	while in the refugee camps, some women from the community became teachers, with some training from the international volunteers in the camps
Compañero	FMLN fighter, companion
Compa	short for *compañero*
Cofradía	confraternity, brotherhood
Delegates of the word	see Celebrant
Department	equivalent to a county
Ecclesiola	Christian group, 'little church'
Formation	training for religious life
Guinda	mass organised flight on foot
Kairos	a moment of truth, opportunity
Machismo	male chauvinism
Maras	street gangs

Masas	people who accompanied the guerrillas
Medellín	used to refer to the Latin American Bishops' Conference in Medellín, Colombia, in 1968
Muchachos	the guerrillas were popularly know by this term, translated as 'the boys'
Profession/final profession	ceremony of the taking of religious vows
Puebla	used to refer to the Latin American Bishops' Conference in Puebla, Mexico, in 1979
Realidad	a concept that in Spanish goes beyond the literal English translation of 'reality' or 'situation'. *Realidad* includes the notion of the present situation but also the historical developments which have contributed to it.
Rezadora	official prayer lady
Rezo	prayer service
The 14 Families	the families generally supposed to own most of the resources in El Salvador

Acronyms and Abbreviations

ARENA	Alianza Republicana Nacionalista (Nationalist Republican Alliance)
BEC	base ecclesial community
CCR	Comité de la Coordinación de Comunidades y Repoblaciones de Chalatenango (Coordinating Committee of Communities and Resettlements of Chalatenango)
CEBES	Comunidades Eclesiales de Base de El Salvador (Base Ecclesial Communities of El Salvador)
CELAM	Consejo Episcopal Latinoamericano (Latin American Bishops' Conference)
CEPROR	Centro de Promoción Rural (Rural Development Centre)
CIIR	Catholic Institute for International Relations
COM	Coordinación de Organismos de Mujeres (Coordination of Women's Organisations)
CONAMUS	Coordinación Nacional de Mujeres Salvadoreñas (National Coordination of Salvadorean Women)
CRIPDES	Comité Cristiano Pro-Desplazados de El Salvador (Christian Committee for the Displaced in El Salvador)
The Dignas	Mujeres por la Dignidad y la Vida (Women for Dignity and Life)

ERP	Ejército Revolucionario del Pueblo (People's Revolutionary Army) — post-war the Expresión Renovadora del Pueblo (People's Expression of Renewal)
FAL	Fuerzas Armadas de Liberación (Armed Liberation Forces)
FMLN	Frente Farabundo Martí para la Liberación Nacional (Farabundo Martí Front for National Liberation — the Frente)
FPL	Fuerzas Populares de Liberación (Popular Liberation Forces)
FUNDASALVA	Fundación Salvadoreña/Salvadora (Salvadorean Foundation — working with young people with drugs problems)
ICD	International Cooperation for Development, the overseas programme of CIIR
IMC	Iniciativa de Mujeres Cristianas (Christian Women's Initiative)
LADOC	Latin American Documentation (bi-monthly publication of church material, Lima, Peru)
MINUSAL	Mission of the United Nations in El Salvador
MSM	Movimiento Salvadoreño de Mujeres (Salvadorean Women's Movement)
NGO	Non-governmental organisation
ONUSAL	United Nations Observer Mission in El Salvador
ORDEN	Organización Democrática Nacionalista (Democratic Nationalist Organisation — a government anti-subversive paramilitary organisation)
PADECOMSM	Patronato para el Desarrollo de las Comunidades de Morazán y San Miguel (Council for the Development of the Communities of Morazán and San Miguel)
PNC	Policía Nacional Civil (National Civil Police)
PRTC	Partido Revolucionario de los Trabajadores Centroamericanos (Revolutionary Party of Central American Workers)
RN	Resistencia Nacional (National Resistance)
UCA	Universidad Centroamericana José Simeón Cañas (José Simeón Cañas Central American University)
UNICEF	United Nations Children's Fund
UNO	Unión Nacional Opositora (National Opposition Union)
UNTS	Unión Nacional de Trabajadores Salvadoreños (National Union of Salvadorean Workers)

Acknowledgements

Our warm thanks go first to the women who gave so generously of their time and shared their stories with us. Then we remember Carmen Medina, CIIR/ICD's country representative in El Salvador, who suggested contacts, arranged transport, gave us space in her office and general encouragement; Paul Damery, an ICD development worker, who drove us to Suchitoto and Ciudad Segundo Montes; Jon Cortina SJ who arranged our visit to Guarjila and drove us there and back at breakneck speed; Rodolfo Cardenal SJ at the UCA, who briefed us on the situation in the country at the time; the family of Ana Gloria and Mónica, in whose house Marigold stayed; the Sisters of St Clare in San Antonio Abad, who put Pamela up as they had often done before, and the Sisters of St Clare in Gotera, with whom we both stayed after our visit to Segundo Montes; Quaker Peace and Service in London, who allowed Marigold to spend time in El Salvador to work on the project with Pamela; and the Catholic Fund for Overseas Development (CAFOD) for their support and encouragement.

Finally, our grateful thanks are due to the Servite Sisters' Charitable Trust Fund, without whose generous financial support this project would not have been possible.

Marigold Best
Pamela Hussey

To the women of El Salvador,
whose courage, hope and vibrant faith are
an inspiration
for women everywhere

Introduction

The hour is coming, the hour is come, when the vocation of women is being achieved in its fullness, the hour in which women acquire in the world an influence, an effect, a power, never attained until now. This is why at this moment when humanity is undergoing so profound a change, women imbued with the spirit of the Gospel can do so much to save the human race from degradation.

Pope Paul VI, Second Vatican Council, 8 December 1965.

Pope Paul's words came at the close of an inspiring and seminal event, the Second Vatican Council. But what happens when women become involved in a kind of evangelisation, political or social activity, which tries to put that spirit of change into practice? This book reflects the experience of Salvadorean women 'imbued with the spirit of the Gospel'.

On 16 January 1994 we left London for El Salvador. We wanted to meet with and learn from a wide range of women actively engaged in women's issues, and in our three-week visit we talked to more than 30 women individually and in groups, in the towns and in the countryside.

We had both previously spent time in El Salvador. Our work in Britain involved us in trying to support the Salvadorean people as they struggled for human dignity and peace. We were both used to people asking us: 'Don't you come home sad and depressed from seeing so much poverty and hardship?' We would reply that, on the contrary, we came home inspired by the courage and hope of most of the people we met. We saw the flames of the Spirit springing up everywhere; and we wished that we could bring back some glowing embers to share within our own relatively unhopeful society.

This was our underlying desire as we talked to a variety of strong women — the main guardians of these 'glowing embers' — in parishes and communities, in churches, in politics and in the burgeoning women's movement. The result is this book, an anthology of our conversations with women. We have interspersed these with supporting material which clarifies the women's stories and gives an idea of the strength of the forces arrayed against them.

Common themes

Included in the supporting material is one of the 'pieces of a portrait' of Archbishop Oscar Romero of San Salvador, collected by María López Vigil in *Piezas para un Retrato*.[1] In the piece Ernestina Rivera, a 'prayer-lady' from Aguilares, refers to Father Rutilio Grande, the Jesuit priest whose murder was such an important factor in transforming Romero into the 'voice of the voiceless'. The year was 1972. More than 20 years later, the issues she raised remain key, and our conversations with Salvadorean women today retain the focus on gospel awakening, conscientisation,[2] empowerment and the price to be paid. In the words of Ernestina Rivera:

> When someone died, it was me people came to. I also said prayers for saints' feast days [...] some days as many as five lots of prayers! [...]
>
> When Father Rutilio Grande and the other Jesuit Fathers arrived in Aguilares with their mission to evangelise, they asked around and they realised that I was someone that everybody knew [...] Only my kids were at home when Father Grande and the others turned up.

---

1. María López Vigil, *Piezas para un Retrato*. San Salvador: UCA Editores, 1993.
2. Conscientisation is a concept developed by the Brazilian educator Paulo Freire which refers to processes of awareness-raising among the poor as part of literacy or post-literacy campaigns. These processes include using political, sociological, cultural, religious and anthropological perspectives. See Paulo Freire, *Pedagogy of the Oppressed*, 1972.

'Is this where the prayer-lady lives, the one they call Señora Tina?' asked Father Rutilio. 'Yes, this is where she lives.'

'And this prayer-lady, is she one of those sky-rockets?' [...]

I couldn't understand why they should have called me such a thing. I was quite upset. When at last I met up with the Jesuit Fathers, they explained that they wanted to evangelise the whole of Aguilares.

'So that people really get to know Christ and the gospel. Do you read the Bible, Tina?' I didn't even have a Bible! I went around with just a handful of prayers. They went on to tell me what their plans were. Finally I said to Father Grande: 'Excuse me, but why did you ask if I was, you know, a sky-rocket?'

'Sky-rockets are the kind of Christians who only point up to the sky, like rockets, the kind that only pray with their eyes gazing up to heaven and don't look at what is all around them and don't care about their neighbours.'

'Well, I have been a bit of a sky-rocket,' I said.

'We'll soon sort that out, Tina. We're relying on you, we need your help because everybody knows you.'

That's how our friendship began. I felt happy, welcome and ready to help them. You know how someone like me, a poor person, blossoms when they feel they count for something. Until then I had thought of priests as so distant, so godlike, that I didn't feel worthy even to talk to them. But with this lot I even began to work on the same level. We began to build communities. Such communities! It all began in Aguilares, that's where everything was born.[3]

Gospel awakening and conscientisation
This anecdote helped us understand our encounters with Rosy, the prayer-lady, and the wake that Pamela attended in San Antonio Abad (page 62), and also the kind of work

---

3. See López Vigil, *op cit.*

that Andrea was doing with the Spanish priests in Jiquilisco
(page 85). But what led up to that joyful, dangerous
blossoming? We came to realise how important Monseñor
Luis Chávez, the Archbishop before Romero, had been in
preparing the seedbed for the blossoming. He had been an
example by defending the right of the poor to organise to
try to improve their lives and by accompanying the people
right to the end of his life. Even after his retirement he
chose to become priest of a parish where two Salvadorean
priests had received death threats and had had to flee the
country.

Archbishop Chávez had encouraged the vocation of
Salvadorean sisters like Noemí (page 55) and Antonia
(page 40) to accompany the poor in life and in death. The
archdiocesan women's programme we visited (page 65) is
the successor to work he started. He supported not only
Salvadorean priests like Rutilio Grande, but also the
Spanish priests Andrea worked with, and the Belgian priest
who inspired Sister Noemí.

As all over Latin America, a large number of foreign
priests and nuns have always lived, and sometimes died,
alongside the Salvadorean people. So it is not surprising
that among the sisters we found 'working on the same
level' in communities now, one was from the Irish
Republic, one from Northern Ireland and two were North
American. Foreigners often find that awakening can work
both ways. In the 1960s, calls went out from Rome to
European religious to go and work in Latin America, to
counteract the influence of 'atheistic communism'. Many of
those who went were converted by the suffering and faith
of the people and became aware that work to transform the
conditions of the poor could not be dismissed as
communism, but was a Christian imperative.

Empowerment
Looking forward from the blossoming in Aguilares, the
shock of the murder of Rutilio Grande in 1977 shows how
helping a community to burst into life can also condemn it

to death: resurrection can lead to death, as well as death to resurrection. A member of the Little Community (page 55), Sister Silvia Arriola, has elsewhere expressed the tragic dilemma, the consequences of women — and the poor and marginalised in general — acquiring 'an influence, an effect, a power, never attained until now':

> Sometimes I think it would have been better not to preach the gospel. If people's consciousness hadn't been raised at least they wouldn't have died [...] I feel deathly sad when I think of all we've done, and how many people committed themselves and now they've been killed.[4]

Blossoming, feeling empowered to try to change their lives, finding in their faith vitamins rather than opium often led to repression and death. Preaching in Aguilares after Rutilio Grande's death, Archbishop Romero said: 'The testimony given by the people of Aguilares is an example to all the parishes in the country ' No wonder those in power wanted to crush such blossoms.

The price paid

Señora Tina was one of the women able to 'bring God close to the people', which Noemí felt was one of women's special gifts. Her involvement in evangelisation led her into building communities, perhaps into working with popular organisations or a political party. She must surely, if she survived, have faced persecution, been forced into the hills with the guerrillas or fled as a refugee. Now, in a time of 'peace', is she finding — like so many women we met who had contributed, and suffered, so much before and during the civil war — that her development as a woman is blocked in the home, in the church and in politics — by *machismo* and hierarchical structures? Is she even experiencing what Nelly del Cid describes (page 20) as 'the bitterness of a

---

4. Sister Silvia Arriola, quoted in Pablo Galdámez, *Faith of a People. The life of a base Christian community in El Salvador.* London: CIIR, 1986.

"useless suffering"', the disillusion many expressed to us about how little seems to have been gained by all the years of anguish?

Keeping hope alive

It is hard for us in Britain to imagine living through the horrors that most of the women you will meet in this book experienced during the years of war, or coming through such tragedy so full of spiritual strength. Sadly, but perhaps not surprisingly, they found it easier to feel God close to them, and to feel close to one another, in the communal struggle against military repression than they do in the increasingly individualistic struggle they now face for economic survival. As Nelly del Cid says: 'The [...] economic situation is so [...] stifling that it is exiling the God of Life.'[5]

The people who spent the war years in guerrilla-controlled zones of El Salvador, or in refugee camps in Honduras or Nicaragua, had not only had a vision of a more humane society. They had had some experience of beginning to build it, developing education, healthcare and community structures even amidst war or exile. They, and the many international agencies who tried to assist such development, hoped that the communities would be able to use their experience to contribute to building a more humane society in post-war El Salvador. This hope has proved unrealistic. The promised land seems as far away as ever.

We must not forget, however, that the women who had glimpsed that vision, and whose stories make up the bulk of this book, represent only a conscientised minority in El Salvador. Thousands of women, particularly in the cities, experienced the war mainly as something that made their daily struggle to make ends meet and to keep their families going even more difficult. Their main source of information was often the ultra-rightwing media, which blamed every

---

5. Nelly del Cid, 'El Salvador: Discovering a God who hides himself', in *The Way*, January 1996.

problem on the guerrillas. Children like Mónica (page 179) were taught at school that Archbishop Romero was murdered by a guerrilla. Teenage girls idolised the man responsible for that murder, Major Roberto D'Aubuisson, and filled scrapbooks with photos and eulogies of him when he died. On the fourth anniversary of D'Aubuisson's death, masses were said in 17 Catholic churches 'to give thanks for his life and hold him up as a model for Salvadorean youth'.

At the same time, most people have had experiences which make them mistrust and fear the police and other authorities, but they have been filled with an even greater fear of those whom even now they automatically call 'the subversives'. So they take no part in any activity which might be called 'political'. All the resilience, and often spiritual strength too, which they share with their conscientised sisters goes into finding ways to survive the economic pressures and ubiquitous violence. They just hope that somehow things will get better.

Keeping hope alive is also the most important task identified by the women's groups in this period of disorientation and depression (pages 144, 148). 'We are not going to allow ourselves to be dispirited,' Isabel Ascencio told Marigold in November 1994, when she was in El Salvador again. She was speaking of the deep disappointment felt after the March election results (see note on page 45). 'El Salvador at the moment is like a huge hospital with many sick and wounded. We in the Christian base communities are sick too, but not so gravely. Those of us who are less sick must help those who are more sick.' This may mean concentrating on slow, small scale grassroots work, based on remembering and understanding the past, keeping a vision for the future, but always rooted in the reality of where people are at the present moment. That may include seeking a deeper understanding of the popularity of the charismatic sects that, superficially, may appear to be 'sky-rockets'.

Claiming dignity

A basic aim of grassroots work is to strengthen women's feeling of 'counting for something', like Señora Tina in Aguilares, and therefore possessing dignity. We found the concept of dignity at the heart of the claims of all the women we met. It is something on which women working in the home, in the church, in politics or in the women's movement can unite, a concept difficult to 'satanise' in the way Mercedes Cañas told us feminism had been satanised (page 153). The Dignas (Women for Dignity and Life) exemplify the attempt to overcome sectarian divisions and encourage women of all backgrounds to work together for their right to be respected in every sphere of life. No longer content to slot into the roles assigned by a male-dominated family, church or political system, they rely on the development of their own potential as women to show them the way forward. They learn from their experience in real life rather than toeing any kind of ideological line. One might liken them to Sister Peggy O'Neill, not wanting to be caught in a systematised 'liberation theology' but seeking to 'collide with God in the real world' (page 102).

Creative rethinking is going on at all levels within the Salvadorean women's movement as well as among many people outside the country who identify deeply with the fate of the Salvadorean people. Acknowledging our sisterhood with the women of El Salvador is important for supporting them in their struggle to change their society, but also for helping us to change our own. The Board of the Washington-based Religious Task Force on Central America, in a reflection on the challenges facing solidarity work today, said:

> In our own society we have seen the emergence of an incredible politics of meanness and selfishness. We now live in a political climate in which there is a loss of a sense of the common good. [...] Unless this country changes, unless we can get to the roots of who we are as

a society and why we do what we do, real change in the quality of life for Central Americans and all the poor of our world will remain distant.[6]

The Salvadorean people have not (or not yet) been able to fulfil the dreams for the future which we share with them. The intensity with which so many of us identify with those dreams shows how deeply they are also our dreams, also still unfulfilled. Just as much as the Salvadoreans, we need what Nelly del Cid called a growing 'spirituality of resistance' to the dominant ideology which tries to persuade us all that there is no alternative. We hope that, like us, after reading these stories you will agree with her that 'it is a privilege to drink from the well of the experience and faith of a people. It motivates one to stay with them in the fight for life.'[7] Cherishing the memory of past blossoming, and of those who died to produce it, is essential for nourishing new seedbeds and breathing new life into dull embers. We feel sure that the extraordinary women who shared their stories with us will be led by the Spirit into new flowering and new flames. Any flowers and flames that we can produce will strengthen them as they have for so long strengthened us.

---

6. *Central America Report*, December 1994.
7. Del Cid, 1996, *op cit*.

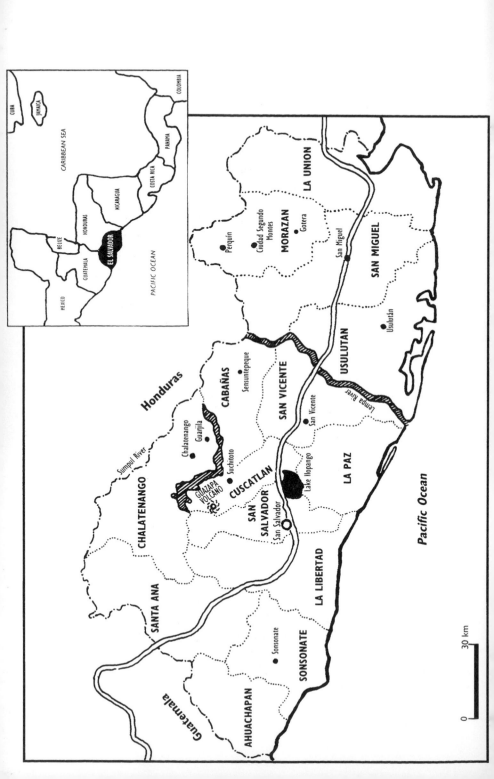

El Salvador
Historical background

El Salvador is the most densely populated country in Latin America: about the size of Wales, it has a population of more than 5 million. Two per cent of the population own 60 per cent of the land; 60 per cent of the people who live in the countryside are landless. More than half the population cannot meet basic food and medical needs. Forty-seven per cent of children suffer from malnutrition. The illiteracy rate is very high.

The Farabundo Martí Front for National Liberation (FMLN) was named after Farabundo Martí, the leader of the 1932 rebellion of peasants, mainly coffee-pickers, who rose up in desperation when their wages were halved. Thirty land-owners were killed in the short-lived insurrection, but between 20,000 and 30,000 peasants were slaughtered in cold-blooded reprisals.

In 1980, after years of fruitless peaceful attempts to change an unjust social and political system, war broke out between the FMLN and the government. Seventy-five thousand people died in the 12 years of conflict, most of them civilians killed by government forces and death squads. About 1 million Salvadoreans took refuge outside the country, while another half million were displaced inside. Refugees began returning to El Salvador to resettle in 1987.

The Peace Accords
On 16 January 1992, at Chapultepec, Mexico, the government of El Salvador and the FMLN signed peace accords which were the culmination of a long process of negotiation brokered by the United Nations. The complex negotiations had begun in Geneva in April 1990 and were about more than ending the war. They were also about creating a

democratic and demilitarised state in El Salvador, which required fundamental changes to the constitution. The two sides began from diametrically opposed positions and over the years reached agreements affecting every area of national life, including human rights, land, and social and economic issues.

In his speech at Chapultepec, President Alfredo Cristiani of the ruling party, the Nationalist Republican Alliance (ARENA), acknowledged the 'profound social and political roots' of the war:

Now democracy belongs to everyone without exclusion or privileges. The agreement is an act of freedom for an entire people whose suffering and stoicism have given it the supreme right to hope for a more humane life.[8]

FMLN commander Schafik Handal affirmed: 'From now on the entire nation will be the protagonist of its own transformation.'[9]

In 1992 CIIR wrote that 'for the Salvadorean people, especially the poor majority, there is the prospect, after 12 years of war and terrible suffering, of an end to the fighting and the promise of a more just society. D-day, 1 February 1992 the formal beginning of the ceasefire, brought them out in force nationwide, in a surge of joy and hope that for that day at least overcame fear.'[10]

Sadly, these bright hopes did not translate into reality.

The FMLN entered the political arena and contested the 1994 elections, from which it emerged as the second largest political force in the country after ARENA, which had been returned to power under the presidency of Armando Calderón Sol. El Salvador in 1994 was still far from seeing the full implementation of the accords. The majority still suffered social and economic exclusion: the government clung to neoliberal economic policies; political space was

---

8. *Step by Step Towards Peace in El Salvador. A chronology of the negotiations.* London, CIIR, 1992.
9. Ibid.
10. Ibid.

lacking; violence, repression and violations of human rights continued; and impunity guaranteed freedom from conviction and punishment for the perpetrators of violence.

Schafik Handal's ringing declaration came to nothing: the majority of Salvadoreans have not participated in the rebuilding of the country. They have been marginalised and ignored, even by some of those in the FMLN from whom they had most right to expect firm indications of a better future.

A profound sense of disillusionment, even betrayal, replaced the joyful optimism of Chapultepec. This was compounded by bitter infighting in the FMLN. Groups which had looked to the FMLN for direction and inspiration, among them many women's groups and base ecclesial communities (BECs), began to dissociate themselves from any political affiliation and to declare their autonomy.

El Salvador today
This was the prevailing mood of the country when we visited in January 1994. Two years later the situation has, if anything, deteriorated. The people are poorer. Violence is worse than it was during the war, with an average of 21 murders a day (as of February 1996). Delinquency is spreading fear among the population at every level and the National Civil Police (PNC), set up by the peace accords to remedy the abuses of the old security forces, is showing signs of emulating their violent methods. Reform of the judicial system has been partial: the process of cleaning up the judiciary, in accordance with UN recommendations, began only in December 1994, since when 40 judges have been dismissed on charges ranging from incompetence to corruption.

ARENA is once again the party in power. President Armando Calderón Sol responds to the interests of powerful economic groups and seems unable to handle the social unrest generated by laws and a socio-political system which make life so difficult for the poor majority. Workers have no mechanism to express their demands other than

13

demonstrations and public protests, which are often violently terminated by the PNC. Those who join trade unions risk losing their jobs, and so are obliged to put up with unjust and unhealthy working conditions and minimal pay. The opposition parties on the left seem not to have noticed how the social sectors which supported them feel deceived by their performance, especially in the National Assembly, where they are seen voting for ARENA's plans. The bulletin *Proceso*, published by the Jesuit-run Central American University (UCA), commented on this blindness of the left: 'We hope that when they do realise the gravity of the situation, it is not too late.'[11]

In 1992 the United Nations Security Council adopted Resolution 729 (1992) by which it decided 'to enlarge the mandate of the United Nations Observer Mission to El Salvador (ONUSAL) to include the verification and monitoring of the implementation of all the [peace] agreements once these are signed in Mexico City'. Failure to achieve full implementation of the agreements led to the UN repeatedly extending its stay in the country. This was due to terminate on 30 April 1996, but a small office stays on, possibly until December 1996, to oversee the implementation of the remaining recommendations of the peace accords: the land transfer programme, the resettlement camps, constitutional reforms, and problems relating to public security.

In May 1996 *Proceso* commented:

> The peace accords and international verification, even reduced to their minimum expression, represent an historic opportunity to consolidate the peace. This opportunity has not been taken full advantage of owing to the resistance displayed by the government, by ARENA and the extreme right. And also owing to the weakness of the United Nations.[12]

---

11. *Proceso*, 6 December 1995.
12. *Proceso*, 2 May 1996.

Archbishops of San Salvador

The last three archbishops of San Salvador have been remarkable men.

Luis Chávez

Monseñor Luis Chávez y González, the third archbishop of San Salvador, led the archdiocese from 1938 to 1977. Even before the Second Vatican Council (1962-65), his main concern was to keep the Salvadorean church in step with the times. He used to say that from every meeting outside El Salvador he brought back something to modernise his pastoral action. Under his leadership the Salvadorean church reached out to the rural population for the first time in its history. Thousands of peasants were trained as pastoral agents and defenders of human rights. Cooperatives were started, and the church began to concern itself with the problem of the political exclusion of significant sectors of Salvadorean society. It saw that if the socio-economic marginalisation of peasant communities was ignored, it risked harbouring the seeds of future conflict. Base ecclesial communities began to develop. The women's religious congregations were asked to organise visits to rural areas, to take the people the good news of the kingdom. This 'insertion into reality' was to have a permanent effect on the congregations themselves and on the Salvadorean church. A rural development centre (CEPROR) ran special courses for young women and trained them in community work.

Archbishop Chávez's auxiliary was Monseñor Arturo Rivera Damas, who for nearly two decades helped him introduce into the Salvadorean church the teaching of the Second Vatican Council (1962-65) and the conclusions of the 1968 Latin American Bishops' Conference at Medellín,

Colombia (see box). Rivera had made enemies, who dubbed him 'the red bishop', so it was not surprising — although deeply resented by those sectors of the church faithful to Vatican II and Medellín — that it was the conservative Oscar Romero who was appointed archbishop when Luis Chávez died in 1977.

Oscar Romero
Romero began his work as archbishop of San Salvador in February 1977. Three weeks later the murder of his friend, the Jesuit Rutilio Grande, together with an old man and a

---

Meetings of Latin American Bishops

The first General Conference of Latin American bishops was held in Rio de Janeiro, Brazil, in 1955 and led to the setting up of a permanent structure, the Latin American Bishops' Conference (CELAM).

The second General Conference at Medellín, Colombia, in 1968 proved to be a watershed in the history of the church in Latin America. At Medellín, the bishops denounced the unjust system which kept the majority of the region's people in a state of poverty and oppression. They chose sides firmly, making a 'preferential option for the poor'.

At the third General Conference in Puebla, Mexico, in 1979, the bishops were divided between those who wanted a reaffirmation of Medellín, and those who were disturbed by post-Medellín developments (often labelled 'Marxist') and wanted a return to more 'religious' matters. The direction taken at Medellín was confirmed but not without a struggle.

Conservative pressure supported by the Vatican was even stronger at the fourth General Conference, held in Santo Domingo in 1992, the 500th anniversary of the so-called discovery of America. Despite the conservative challenge, the bishops at Santo Domingo reaffirmed their commitment to the poor, and pledged the church to work for the promotion of women and develop a new relationship with indigenous and African-American cultures.

boy who were with him, completed the 'conversion' which his contact with the popular organisations and the base communities had begun.

Romero nurtured the seed sown by Luis Chávez: the church's commitment to the Salvadorean people developed from being one of support and encouragement to firm backing for the economic and political demands of popular organisations. He promoted discussion of politics and human rights, and took up the cause of women in the church, continuing the pastoral line of Archbishop Chávez by encouraging the sisters to share the lives of the poor.

Romero's outspoken defence of the people and denunciation of the evils of Salvadorean society at all levels was the immediate cause of his assassination on 24 March 1980, at the hands of a killer hired by the founder of the ARENA party, Roberto D'Aubuisson, now known to have been closely linked to the death squads.

Arturo Rivera Damas

After the murder of Archbishop Romero, Rivera was named apostolic administrator of the Archdiocese. He remained in this position for three years, before the Vatican appointed him archbishop of San Salvador. This is some indication of the division within the church itself with respect to the pastoral activity of both Archbishop Romero and Monseñor Rivera.

Monseñor Rivera, it has been said, experienced the awakening of the poor in El Salvador — an awakening which cost them dear, as the testimonies of the women in this book make clear. He saw the people develop a sense of their own dignity and take responsibility for their history. He witnessed the terrible repression and the great migrations of refugees and displaced people. Finally, he encouraged the dialogue and negotiations which brought the war to an end with the signing of peace accords in Mexico in January 1992.

> Monseñor Chávez, Monseñor Romero and Monseñor Rivera were not only great pastors and religious leaders, they also by their presence decisively influenced the historical process of El Salvador in the second half of the 20th century. And they did this to the benefit of the majority of Salvadoreans, those who wanted a greater justice, equality and freedom. This makes them true heroes and patriots of El Salvador, that is, true founding fathers of the Salvadorean nation in the process of gestation.[13]

We met Archbishop Rivera in February 1994, when he told us that the archbishopric was constantly under attack from the right-wing daily *El Diario de Hoy*. The paper had mounted a mud-slinging campaign against his auxiliary bishop, Gregorio Rosa Chávez, who had two brothers in the FMLN. Monseñor Rivera much regretted the polarisation during the 1994 election campaign between the government and the opposition parties, which did not augur well for the future. Before we left, at his request, we took a photograph of him standing next to a bust of Monseñor Romero.

Just over a month later, in a homily delivered on 6 March, Rivera announced that the process of beatification of archbishop Oscar Romero would begin on 24 March, the 14th anniversary of his death. In the same homily, referring to the approaching presidential elections, Rivera appealed to the people to vote thinking of the future, and asked how this could be done by supporting those who did not take the peace accords seriously, and who had murdered Monseñor Romero.

Monseñor Rivera died of a heart attack on 26 November 1994. This touched us deeply. *Proceso* commented in an appreciation written after his death that it was no wonder that Monseñor Rivera had the same enemies as Monseñor Chávez and Monseñor Romero.

---

13. *Proceso*, 22 March 1995.

The sixth archbishop

On 21 April 1995 Bishop Fernando Sáenz Lacalle, auxiliary bishop of Santa Ana and bishop to the armed forces, was named archbishop of San Salvador. Bishop Gregorio Rosa Chávez, whom many had thought might be named the new archbishop, continued as auxiliary bishop of the archdiocese. The appointment of Bishop Sáenz Lacalle, a Spaniard and a member of the right-wing Opus Dei movement, was welcomed by the government, which hoped he would 'return the Catholic church to its true role'. In one of his first pronouncements, the new archbishop said: 'The mistakenly named liberation theology [...] is a re-reading of the *New Testament* in Marxist code and has a tendency to generate violence, which is something that no longer has a place in El Salvador.'

It remains to be seen how far the new archbishop will depart from the pastoral model created and fostered by his three predecessors. He has said that he shares their commitment to the eradication of poverty; whether he shares their commitment to the poor is another matter.

Carmen Manuela del Cid

The implications of Christian commitment were presented to us by Carmen Manuela del Cid, Nelly, a young Honduran preparing a thesis on feminist theology at the Central American University (UCA), and doing theology by working with marginalised communities.

Marigold Best: When we come to El Salvador we are always moved and strengthened by your faith and hope, and the spirit you show in working together for a better future. We come from a country where many people now feel little hope and wonder what has gone wrong with our society. Many of our worries are similar to those you have here: growing poverty and unemployment; increasing violence, especially against women; damage to the environment; materialism and consumerism; the focus on the individual and neglect of the community. We also feel that in our country there is a great hopelessness and spiritual poverty, a feeling that we can't change anything. Perhaps your example can help us to try and revive some flames of hope.

Nelly: When you were talking, two pictures came into my mind: one of a society abundant in material goods, the other a society full of material want. In both there is terrible violence. In the picture of abundance, the individual seems to be all-important and is like an island, independent of those around him or her. But this individual hasn't got everything, and may have hidden needs. People with needs can either withdraw into themselves or open up to each other. In the first picture, the people involved seem to be closed in within the family, in a little exclusive world. In the second picture, here in the poorest war-torn rural communities, for example, people know that if they do not stay together they will all die. Unity means the possibility of surviving. The family is important here, but there is a closer relationship between the wider community and the family community.

Loss of community spirit

The marginal communities here in the city are something else altogether. Many of them come from the countryside and are lost in the city. They are not welcome here and it is a struggle to live, so community values disappear. There is extreme deprivation, together with theft and drug addiction. Everything is related to the loss of values, including that of community spirit. When everyone is fighting for survival, it is difficult for neighbours to be friends. They are always quarrelling. But there are little oases in this desert where there is hope among those who have managed to keep the values. They are able to make a commitment, and when they begin to organise they are capable of giving more than could be imagined. But here comes a contradiction — that at this level of survival people always trust in God. For example, when they go out to steal many of them will say: 'Please God, let it all go well'. Why? They may steal, even threaten with a knife, but for many this is the only way they can survive. Are they guilty? No. The system has trapped them to such an extent that they cannot develop. They have the right to steal, because others take from them what they need.

You will see many contradictions here. For instance, here in San Salvador there are plenty of shops, restaurants and light, modern buildings. But there are other parts of the city which are hidden because walls are being built to isolate them, so that visitors will not notice them. But they cannot really be hidden. The cholera epidemic,[14] for example, has shown up the appalling health system in this country, where the people haven't got the necessary conditions to keep healthy. On television they are told to boil the

---

14. Ana Gloria (page 176) contracted cholera while we were there but had quick access to hospital and was cured. People in rural areas do not have such access.

water, to wash their hands when they go to the latrine, and a whole list of things. But people very often have no access to running water, and boiling it takes a great deal of wood for a big family. Wood is expensive in the city and the water they get is contaminated. So there is no way they can act on the advice they are given. This is the great imbalance in our society. But in spite of everything the people remain hopeful.

Role reversal

I am going to tell you a little story. As a religious sister, I used to live in a house lent to me by my congregation. When the time came for me to leave, I couldn't find another house and I became a bit desperate. The San Rafael community, most of whom are women on the margins of survival, managed to find me a little house near them. The solidarity of these people was wonderful. They came to collect my things, helped me move and when I was settled in they arranged a thanksgiving prayer in which they included all those who had nowhere to live. They identified with me because they had experienced similar upheavals and desperation. So we felt closer to each other, more united. I felt it was a reversal of roles: for a time it was I, the pastoral worker, who supported the community, but now it is the community that is supporting me, and teaching me how to live in insecurity. They are experts in insecurity, living under constant threat of eviction and in appalling conditions. You could say that they are specialists at knowing how to put their lives into God's hands.

'A God who walks with them'

This could be the First World's problem: that having too much security in other things, they think God is unnecessary. But where nothing is certain, where people are constantly under threat, there is only one being who gives security, and that is God. No matter how bad things are — if the house collapses, if their child is ill and facing death — people know that God is still there with them.

These people possess a sense of nomadic spirituality such as the Israelites had in the beginning. We have lost this because we have become too settled. They haven't lost it because they are always expecting to move on. They discover a God who walks with them, and so they can also identify with a small God, a God who hasn't got an answer to everything, a God who is so weak that he suffers with them. But he is a God who is with them, there, and when they discover this more clearly, they become capable of greater commitment. They discover that there are things that need to be changed. It always used to be said that people should resign themselves to God's will. Many people live in this resignation, feeling that God is near, but that he doesn't care. But when their faith begins to mature and they discover that their situation is not God's will, they take a leap forward to find a God who has, as they used to say in Morazán, come among them, who has identified with them, who was crucified. In a workshop for pastoral workers, all peasants, we were discussing why Jesus was killed. Their answer was, 'they killed him for being a big-mouth', for speaking out and denouncing injustice, for saying that God wanted to be called Father by everybody. When people realise that this God, this Jesus, is a 'big-mouth' they can identify with him more closely, because he is not asking them to be passive. They also know that he won't change things from above; they have to make the commitment and change things from where they are, so that God's kingdom can come.

Building a different world

It is here that the great discovery sometimes takes place — the centrality of God's kingdom. What is this kingdom if not a world, a society, where we can live like true human beings, true children of God? When this central fact is discovered, you realise that it is not a question of praying, lighting candles or taking part in Holy Week — but of committing yourself to building a different world, and this is done day by day, with small acts.

In the marginalised community of San Rafael, they know that to commit themselves to the kingdom is to be ready to help their neighbour in however small a way — so that, for example, if someone who can't read needs to obtain a particular document, another member of the community who can read goes with her. It is a readiness to be at the service of others. Another small example is that of an old woman on her own, whose house was going to collapse on her. The community came, demolished the house, organised matters and built the house up again.

Ideological bombardment

It is not caring for others that has to change. It is a great struggle, because we are surrounded by this ideology that 'nobody matters but me'. This is very strong, particularly now that the war is over. The ideological bombardment through radio and television is brutal. It has even affected those communities that were the most organised and did more collective work. Formerly the government could not reach them, and now it does through institutions that want to implant the ideology of private enterprise and encourage the growth of small businesses. This isn't bad, but in the countryside, for instance, the system breaks down because there is a conflict between collective and individual interests. The older people, those over 30, are more for the communitarian way of life, and they are the poorest — they know they can't manage on their own, they need the community. But the younger ones, the under-30s, who are getting all the training that has begun since the war, they are all for the individual. There is a different mentality: the system is about the individual and nothing but the individual. This is a big problem in the First World and here it is beginning to be a problem. The government is conquering us ideologically, alienating us, taking away our right to be ourselves. People in Chalatenango have said to me: 'We produce here, we make shoes, we have a dressmaking workshop, but the people here don't want to buy. Why? Because they prefer what comes from abroad, with a trademark and a name.' That is how they are winning over the people. How to fight this is a great challenge, for the First World as well as for us. The First World wants to conquer us, and by giving us its ideology can go on enjoying what belongs to everyone. The great challenge is not to deny the individual, but to find the right balance between the individual and the community, and to identify how to relate the two.

Women's place
Pamela Hussey: What do you think of the place of women in church and society?

Nelly: We have a clearer awareness now of our position. Many of the women's groups here in El Salvador began as offshoots of the Frente [FMLN]. The first aim was not to help women but to help the Frente. But now a further step is being taken. During the war women helped in many ways: as combatants, in logistics, making *tortillas*, working in safe houses in the city, looking after the wounded. They played a very important role, but this was not recognised. Nonetheless, women managed to express themselves in a way they could not do previously.

During the war many issues were postponed; everything had to wait until afterwards. But the war ended and there is no 'afterwards'. Many women's organisations have now broken with the Frente — not a complete break, but simply saying: 'Now we are going to work for ourselves on gender issues, finding our own identity, and discovering what special contribution only we can make.' All this has been reinforced by the international women's movement. The work at international, Latin American and Central American levels has supported the task of explaining why women were always inferior, why they always had to carry out the domestic tasks and why their issues were considered unimportant and their voices were not heard. All these questions lead to answers: women begin to find themselves and their voice. A Latin American theologian has said:

'Women are making the fascinating discovery of not knowing their place.' Before, the greatest compliment was to say of a woman: 'She knows her place'. But now she is beginning not to know her place, not to allow herself to be told: 'Your place is your home and your children'.

The church as institution

People's attitude towards the church has changed. Previously, church meant a big institution, and when there was no community the people went to the church in Santa Tecla. But when the ecclesial communities began there was more gathering together to reflect on the word. In this way they discovered another meaning of church: how good it is to be together, to be able to share what the word is saying to each of us. They begin to make comparisons. A Mass is not the same as a celebration of the word. In the Mass everything is on a big scale, the priest talks and talks, and we cannot make any comments. Here in the community, on the other hand, we can say what we think. It is another level of relationship. We discover that church is also the small community — the small community is much more church than the big institution. So people begin to give things their right place.

Take the priest, for example. Before, whatever he said was sacrosanct and had to be obeyed. Now, in a sense people are beginning to disown an authority that is at a distance from them — a priest who seldom goes near them, and when he does it is only to scold, even to insult them with hard words. They begin to disown that authority, and to feel more confident in themselves and in their faith. No one need manage their faith for them — they can. So there is a development, they begin to ask questions.

In San Rafael, most people do not go to our parish meetings because they feel that they do not achieve anything, but those who do go dare to say to the priest: 'You don't come to our communities, so how can you say those things of us?' Or: 'We don't agree with what you are saying, because in the community we live in such-and-such a way.' They dare. The fact that they are together, that they reflect on the word of God together, gives them the authority to say something, and to find he is a human being like us. It is a process — people go at different paces, but some have taken the step, and when they do, I think they feel more adult. The church has for a long time wanted to keep women, and the laity in general, in a state of childhood. It has not allowed them the right to be adults in their faith. People meeting around the word of God discover what it says to their life, and learn to see their lives in the light of the word and the word in the light of their lives.

As I see it, it is not just by chance that in Latin America they have been taking the Bible away from the people. In the 1970s, the movement and fervour that followed Medellín and Puebla [see box on page 16] provoked a big effort to get the Bible to the people, who accepted it hungrily. Many communities met around the Bible. This brought about considerable political opposition, because people began to think, to ask questions, to say: 'So, this is not right'. The authorities took fright, being unprepared for this. They were the ones who had always told the people what to do, how the laity should behave, how people should communicate. Suddenly they found that the situation had changed. So they began to take the Bible out of the hands of the people. There are now no projects that provide Bibles, and a Bible that used to cost 10 or 15 *colones* today costs 100 *colones*.[15] People can't afford that. I see all this as a government strategy: having people grow up and take responsibility for their faith does not suit the political structure.

But this has to be the way forward: that people take responsibility for their faith and no longer wait for guidance from the top. This is something that I think has to be pushed even in first world countries. There are too many anonymous individuals. Not so much here, because poverty brings us together, and we rediscover each other.

---

15. 8 *colones* = 1US$, 1994.

This helps us to make small cracks in the system that crushes us and denies us the right to be ourselves. This is as valid for the First World as for the Third.

The Spirit is feminine

The Spirit is the great forgotten one. The Spirit is feminine, and because it is feminine, very close, very tender and very creative. The authorities are frightened of this Spirit and want to control it too. One of the great sins of the Catholic church is that it is very far from the Spirit.

There are new winds blowing — I don't know where they come from or where they are going, but I keep finding other people who feel the same, longing for change and perceiving it. It's a current, and that current, if it is pushing towards life, is the Spirit. It renews, it changes. That leap that people are taking in the small community, discovering themselves as subjects of the faith, that is the work of the Spirit. It couldn't come from anywhere else. It is a meeting with the dream of God. Who but the Spirit could help us to rediscover the forgotten kingdom? As John said: 'The Spirit will lead you', and it's true, it guides us. They don't know how it has happened, but suddenly the people have discovered their potential for life. The people begin from life, in that life where they are continually threatened. From that threatened life they discover the force of the Spirit pushing them to fight for life. As Casaldáliga says: 'It's a fight unto death for life.'[16] It is the Spirit who is pushing, carrying, giving the strength for an ever greater commitment, strength to dare. In a small community some people can be too frightened to open their mouths the first time in a meeting, but after two or three or four, when they have dared to speak for the first time, the action of the Spirit is there, giving the courage to dare.

This is what we in Latin America are discovering in the church of the poor, that to feel oneself to be church doesn't depend on belonging to a particular denomination. It's

---

16. Pedro Casaldáliga, Bishop of São Féliz do Araguaia in Brazil, has a deep pastoral concern for the poor and is a familiar figure in El Salvador.

much wider than that. Church is everything that is in line with the dream of Jesus, which takes on his dream, makes that dream its own, fights for it, is capable of giving one's life for it. That is what belonging to a church means — Catholic, evangelical, or even unbeliever, it doesn't matter. But if someone believes in life and in the life we all deserve, and is filled with the dream of Jesus — that is church. Nothing to do with structures. And one begins to make the fascinating discovery of disowning authorities. One's ultimate obedience is not to an often dictatorial hierarchy, but always to what is life-giving. As Monseñor Romero used to say: 'The smallest and greatest good is life itself.'[17] This is where we are really one — we are beyond denominations here.

---

17. Oscar A Romero, *Voice of the Voiceless: The four pastoral letters and other statements of Archbishop Oscar Romero.* London: CAFOD/CIIR, 1985.

A new way of being church
San Antonio Abad

The parish of San Antonio Abad is a poor neighbourhood on the western outskirts of San Salvador, nestling under the San Salvador volcano.

In the 1970s the parish had been putting into practice the guidelines worked out at the 1968 Latin American Bishops' Conference in Medellín, Colombia. The faith, hope and commitment of the people were growing and hundreds were taking an active part in the life of the community. It was the springtime of the Christian communities, they said, like the first success of Jesus in Galilee.

The neighbourhood became notorious in 1979 when a young priest and four young men were murdered. On 20 January Father Octavio Ortiz was conducting a training weekend in El Despertar, the community centre of the parish. An army unit burst into the compound, shot Father Ortiz dead, drove a tank over his head and murdered four of the young men who were following the course for pastoral leaders. The people abandoned El Despertar. They were too terrified to go back until years later.

The Sisters of St Clare

A Franciscan order founded by St Francis and St Clare in 1253, the Sisters of St Clare, known locally as the Clarisas, established a small community in El Salvador in 1972, in fidelity to their long tradition of solidarity with the poor. They began in the town of Gotera, in the department of Morazán in the east of the country (a zone of intense fighting during the war). In the early 1980s a second community was set up in the capital. When this house was destroyed in the 1986 earthquake, the sisters moved to San Antonio Abad.

The cross and the resurrection

Quantitatively there seems to be more of the cross in our country than resurrection. But qualitatively, it can't be denied without falling into falsehood that there is hope, freedom, self-giving, joy and celebration. And [...] when all these things are real, then there is resurrection too. What we have learnt in these years in El Salvador is that transcendent resurrection is a miracle of God, and living in history as risen people is also a miracle of God. Life continues to have the last word.

Letter to the churches from El Salvador, 16-30 April 1992.
Letter to the Churches is a fortnightly bulletin from the Pastoral Centre of the UCA.

A base ecclesial community
Sister Jean Ryan of the Sisters of St Clare told us of her arrival in the parish of San Antonio Abad in February 1984.

Jean Ryan: A base ecclesial community (BEC) of 700 people had dispersed because of the terrible persecution and massacres that had occurred since 1979. The church had been closed for a few years, and the community centre, El Despertar, had been abandoned and many people from the BEC had fled the area or changed their religion for safety.

A few months before I arrived, a Passionist priest, Father Mando, from the neighbouring parish of Mejicanos, came to celebrate Mass each Sunday at 7am. Very few people came, as on many Sunday mornings a tortured or decapitated body would be left at the church entrance — the work of the death squads.

Sister Otilia of the Little Community [see page 55] and I began to visit houses to invite the people back to Mass. Many of them set their dogs on us: apparently, I looked like the Belgian sister who had worked in the parish before, when they suffered so much repression, so they were not ready to accept me. However, we managed to form a group of six youths for confirmation. They would then become catechists and start teaching small groups of children for first communion. This evangelisation of children was acceptable as long as we didn't start classes with adults!

The arrival of Fathers Michael Campbell-Johnston SJ and Carmelo Eguen SJ in El Despertar really started things moving again. Father Carmelo was to help us Sisters of St Clare at the weekends (we now had charge of the parish). I had already started a celebration of the word every Wednesday night in the parish church, but it was soon looked on with suspicion by the 'authorities' in our church, the Cofradía. Soon the key of the church, which the Cofradía possessed, was refused us, so we looked for a house where the family was prepared to take the risk. It soon became obvious that the group was too big for a small house — about 50 were now coming — and that we would need helpers.

Thus we started what we called bible study to form leaders for the resurrected BEC. Bible study was an umbrella name for the study of the Bible and church documents, especially Medellín, Puebla, *Evangelii Nuntiandi*,[18] and other documents on the social teaching of the church. We always studied these in the context of the current reality of the country. We invited speakers such as the Jesuits Jon Sobrino, Amando López and Juan Ramón Moreno[19] to help us with the theology, and others from human rights groups to explain the social, economic, ecclesial and political reality of the country.

Soon the group grew to about 70 adults, all crammed on to the patio of a house. Most of the people were members of the 'old' community who had suffered persecution, and many, or most, had lost members of their families in the massacres in San Antonio Abad.

With no hope of using the church for our work, as Mass itself was hardly permitted there, and with the people afraid to return to El Despertar, a crisis arose between the

---

18. *Evangelii Nuntiandi* is a 1975 apostolic exhortation of Pope Paul VI on evangelisation in the modern world. In it, he commits the church to the language of liberation.
19. Amando López and Juan Ramón Moreno were two of the six Jesuit priests murdered in El Salvador on 16 November 1989. Jon Sobrino was lecturing in Bangkok at the time and so escaped the massacre.

traditional Cofradía and the BEC. The BEC left the church to celebrate Mass in the street, which we did for a whole year, in sun and rain. Archbishop Rivera closed the church again and threatened the Cofradía with excommunication.

Finally, the community procured a piece of land from the mayor of the city and we built another church. The Sisters of St Clare, with financial help from the German agency Adveniat, built an education and training centre on their grounds. With a place to worship and a place to meet, we divided the parish into 10 sectors. Each sector was a small base community with a celebration of the word each week and a group of catechists to give classes for First Communion. Sister Phyllis started a marriage group which is still going strong, helping new couples prepare themselves for this sacrament and to join the base community. All training of leaders was done together, and from then on we went from strength to strength.

Members of the community talk
One evening Jean arranged for six members of the base ecclesial community to come round to the sisters' house to talk about the community.

Aurelia: The community began in the 1970s and I joined it in 1974, when the Belgian priests came to the pastoral centre, El Despertar [the 'Awakening']. It is called that because those priests came to wake us: we were asleep, we took no notice of the injustices around us. We ignored the fact that the armed forces were at the root of the injustices, not the *muchachos* as they tried to make us believe.

The *muchachos* had to organise to fight the injustice against the people. At the same time we were reading the Bible, which was beginning to wake us: if you read the gospels you wake up, because the gospels help you to analyse. Through the *muchachos* and the Bible we realised that it is not a bad thing to organise, because the *Book of Kings* says that you have to organise to fight injustice.

It is said that some people are rich; but they are

33

materially rich, in spiritual things there are no rich people. So we began to claim the richness of spiritual things. They call us poor, but in material things, not spiritually.

Carmen: I began in the community after my husband and my daughter persuaded me to. I hadn't wanted to go, but when I saw what it was all about I liked it, so I continued going. The community grew and they began to hold study meetings for men, for young people and for us women. It wasn't communism as people said. All of us who were involved in this were called communists, and people were frightened of us.

We continued with the meetings and the community formed a cooperative — it was very good. Then, with the war and the murder of Father Octavio, few of us went to the meetings. We were too afraid. The authorities came to investigate, going into people's houses to see what they had. Books for bible study had to be hidden. I had a picture of Monseñor Romero and I hid it when they came to search. They asked me what was the use of all my papers, and said that it was to learn communism. They caught my children behind the house and asked them where the guns were. They came several times to search. So we withdrew a little from the community, because they said we were communists and we were frightened. They killed many young men and others who belonged to the community — they took them from their houses and they were never heard of again.

Jean: The community is divided into six sectors of about 16 people. Each sector has its celebration of the word during the week. On Sunday we study the Bible, and during the week we share with each sector.

Berta: As we reflect, there are different opinions. Everyone sees the Bible from the perspective of their own life, and also links it to the situation of the country. So many years of war, so much that has happened — and the Bible fits it all, it doesn't just belong to those times, but to today. Each of us starts from our own experiences. Everyone gives different opinions and we all learn.

Husband and wife reflect together

Jean Ryan: A lot of reflection is carried out between couples, looking at the family, the relationship between husband and wife, and children. This has been very enriching.

Milagro: My husband and I are just beginning in the community. We started one afternoon by going to a bible study, because my husband wasn't accepted in the church as he drank a lot. We wanted to get married, despite having been together and with children for quite a few years, and we began to go to talks for couples. My husband said: 'We've been together so long, what are we going to learn?' And yes, we had learned a lot, but we had not reflected on life as a couple. Well, we began, and then Sister Felipa [Phyllis] arrived and asked if we wanted to join the marriage team.

I said: 'No, my husband drinks, and if we were in the group we would have to give testimony, and we wouldn't want to.' She said: 'I always see you together, with the children.' (We have six children.) But she didn't see him during the week when he was drinking, but only on Sundays when no one knew he was a drunk. So she said to me: 'If you don't begin today, you won't ever begin. If you wait for him to get better, he will never get better. You have to begin so that as he commits himself, he will begin to change.' So we did this, and sometimes, in the reflections in sectors, I would say to one of the men: 'Look, use appropriate themes which will speak to him, make an impact.' From time to time he arrived drunk and talked a lot, and we sent him to lie down, but he began to get into it. Now he is very committed to the church and has given up drink.

I have two children who are catechists. We send them to retreats, and this year they began to work in the parish. My young daughter goes to nursery catechetics. But I think doing reflections as a couple and a family is good. We talk and we ask our six kids what they think of us as parents, and we tell them what we think of them. Sometimes they have a lot to say to us. We give talks to other couples too.

Here in San Antonio we have no schools, but we have bars everywhere. I think the government allows this because drunks are incapable of claiming their rights. A drug addict is the same. And television begets violence. We live in a consumer society — that's why people don't want many children. When I tell people I have six, they say: 'Oh! What are you thinking?' But I think each child is a blessing. Before, we had two and we were worse off than we are now. Now we have six, and we live better. They are all studying, they all help in the house, so that they don't grow up with *macho* ideas, which are very common here. Their father helps too — so that each one does their share, and the children see that their father helps in the home too. It's not just talk, he really does it.

Rosa América's story

Rosa América: We meet on Thursdays to reflect on the word. There are about 10 or 11 of us including some young people. We are the fruit of the old community that was here before. I don't come from San Antonio; we came here in 1982. I and my husband used to go to Mass and then straight home. We didn't understand what it meant. But God calls people, he touches people's hearts and we heard Sister Jean inviting people to a bible study, on the *Old Testament*. And the priest who was going to give the study was Father Amando [Amando López, see note 19, page 32]. This made such an impression on me that I said to my husband: 'Let's go to the bible study today.' 'You go,' he said, 'I don't feel like going.'

I didn't know San Antonio very well, because although I had lived there for two years, I didn't go out of my house: I went to Mass and then I buried myself in the house again. But that day it was as if God pushed me, and I came to the bible study, taking my neighbour with me. Thank God she came with me — if she hadn't, I might not have gone. But we gave each other courage. I liked it, because it was then that I began to discover what God wants of each of us, what kind of commitment he wants us to make, and what he is saying to us in the gospel, in each verse. I want the gospel to give us life.

So that is when I began to discover what bible reading was, what we did when we went to Mass, what meaning the Mass had for us. I began to discover all that in the bible reflections. Once I began, I didn't miss a session. Then I began to discover the reason for the struggle of our people: it wasn't only killing but a struggle against the injustices that our friend over there was talking about, and identifying where those injustices came from. The injustices can be seen from the workers claiming their rights, because what they earn for a day's work is miserable. You said your country is very rich, but there are people living in poverty there. It's the same here: here there is money, but the workers and the peasants are asking for land to work — and there isn't any. So the people organised to see where they could work — workers asking for their rights, because they earn nothing. So we begin to discover this through the word of God.

We claim our rights as women — we have to claim them, women should not be marginalised. We are equal to men. We discovered this in our meetings too. God made us equal. I think God pushes a person to commit herself to serve. Thank God, through what we learnt in bible study we gradually persuaded our husbands to reflect too and we managed to keep on going. Our husbands and children came to this community with us. I have three children: my daughter who is nearly 18 and my 16-year-old son are both catechists. We learnt all this from coming to the bible study and sharing with others.

Crisis in the base ecclesial communities
In 1994, on the fifth anniversary of the murder at the UCA of the six Jesuit priests and two women co-workers, people from several base communities met in the Monseñor

Romero Centre of the UCA. They shared their past experiences, their problems and their hopes for the future. They spoke of the values lived by the communities: a selfless love for others, a thirst for justice, a commitment to service, to sharing, and even, for many, to giving one's life. There had also been great hope that, despite problems, they were making progress.

But now they felt that the base communities were in crisis — a crisis of numbers and of their fundamental nature. The basic values were getting weaker, the institutional church was marginalising the communities, and they felt that involvement with political parties had divided the communities.

They needed to rediscover the essential nature of the communities — and to rediscover the gospel. They needed to answer the question: What is God asking of us, the church of the poor, in El Salvador today? Unity had to be rebuilt.

During the war the communities were united around the single goal of changing the unjust social and economic system under which the people had suffered for too long. Many members of the communities joined the armed struggle, seeing it as the only way to bring about change. The unity, however, covered up political divisions which became apparent when peace came. Different communities had links with different 'fronts' of the FMLN during the war, but some now want to be autonomous. They feel that their commitment is to building the kingdom of God and not to a political party, so there are differences with those who want to continue along political lines.

From Oscar Romero's diary:

Sunday 4 March, 1979 *[about six weeks after the murders in El Despertar]*
I went to San Antonio Abad for a meeting with the principal leaders of that community. We studied the situation in depth, discussing with great honesty errors that could lead to great tragedies. We decided that an unwise mixture of politics with pastoral work can cause great evil, and we have agreed that all pastoral workers will keep their pastoral work completely separate from the implications caused by mixing it with political organisations.

Monday 12 March:
I attended a meeting in San Antonio Abad with the leaders of the communities of the different sectors. [...] I think that there is a new resolve to continue, in spite of the difficult situations that have resulted from the murder of Father Octavio and the events at El Despertar.

Saturday 31 March:
I went to San Antonio Abad with the coordinating team of the community. We discussed some of the problematic aspects of this parish where El Despertar is located, which was the site of the murders of Father Octavio and the four young men. We agreed to celebrate a Eucharist on Monday of Holy Week, in the evening, and to install Father Rogelio [Ponceele] in the house, since he will temporarily take charge of the parish until Father Coto, whom the parish is expecting with great affection, is ordained.

Friday 6 April:
[The entry refers to a meeting with the Jesuit Fathers at the Central American University (UCA), where they talked about Romero's forthcoming pastoral letter, 'The mission of the church in the nation's crisis'.]

I want it [the letter] to be about the current problems our archdiocese faces, such as the relationship to the government in a police state and, more importantly, to present a church that wants to be authentic and does not want to ally itself with any political organisation. It tries to understand and support them in so far as their cause is just, but without becoming identified with any of them. And I want to ask all Christians to help build, through our Christian base communities, the true church defined without any ambiguity, clearly the church Christ wants us to build.

From *Archbishop Oscar Romero. A shepherd's diary.* London: CAFOD/CIIR, 1993.

Sisters of St Clare
San Antonio Abad

In 1988, Pamela Hussey spent a month with the Sisters of St Clare, gathering material for a book.[20] At that time there were 13 Sisters of St Clare in El Salvador, four Europeans, one North American, and eight Salvadoreans aged between 20 and 40, most of them from peasant families. They had chosen to join a religious congregation because they felt that this offered them the possibility of a total commitment to the people and their struggle for a more just society.

By the beginning of 1994, only three of the original eight Salvadoreans remained: Antonia, Elvia and Felipa. Two European sisters remain in El Salvador: Jean and Mark. Two others, Anselm and Ann, were in 1994 beginning new work in Guatemala.

Antonia González, the novice mistress, was in 1994 in charge of a full programme of training for four novices: study during the week and at weekends work in a poor parish. Ten young women were hoping to join the congregation: some of them were only finishing primary school, others were doing secondary grades, and one was studying at the university. A year later, eight of these had become novices, and the novitiate had to expand into another house.

Antonia: I knew Monseñor Romero before I became a religious, when he was a young priest working with Monseñor Machado, the bishop in San Miguel. In all the cantons, villages and towns of Morazán he was much appreciated: he was famous for his homilies, for his special gifts of preaching. On special feasts in the cathedral of San Miguel, he, rather than Monseñor Machado, preached. He was always known, too, as a very approachable priest,

---

20. Pamela Hussey, *Free from Fear. Women in El Salvador's church.* London: CIIR, 1989.

someone who was close to the people. He had the gift of simplicity.

I knew him when I was a child of about seven and he used to accompany Monseñor Machado on his visits to the towns, to the cantons, to the communities, doing confirmations. It was funny to see Monseñor Romero (he was Father Romero then) with his fundraising raffles. One day he asked me: 'Do you want to help me sell?', and I said: 'Yes.' So I went off with the tickets and in a little while I sold them, and his comment was: 'You are a little rascal.' From that moment he called me a little rascal, no matter where he met me. Even when I was a religious, he met me somewhere and said: 'If I'm not mistaken, you are the little rascal of Sensembra' (that's my home town). So I said to myself: 'He hasn't forgotten.' That was my first experience of Monseñor Romero.

I also knew his family because his sister-in-law was a teacher, who lived with my family for a time. Then, when I was a religious, I met him again in 1977, when the country was going through a most difficult time. This was when I was with another congregation, before I joined the Sisters of St Clare. They were very good people, but they didn't share my concerns, and I felt shut in. I had to go to San Salvador on one occasion, from Sonsonate, and I went to see Monseñor Romero because I had a lot of confidence in him. I used to speak to him about my concerns, I wanted to find more meaning for my life, but I didn't have the space where I was. He used to make a radio programme, 'Feeling with the church', which I would listen to every day. When the sisters realised that I listened to his programme, they took away my radio. I felt awful.

At that time I had to come into the capital for treatment for my health, and I used to take advantage of the visits to the specialist to go and see Monseñor Romero. I appreciated the sisters; I learnt a lot from them, but I didn't have the space to do something about the things that I felt deeply about. I felt frustrated. I was in a school environment, upper middle class, and it didn't suit me.

I remember a meeting that took place when the persecution was intense. It must have been in early 1977 because Father Tilo[21] hadn't died yet. It was a meeting in the School of the Assumption for all the religious sisters and priests of the archdiocese, because Monseñor Romero wanted to know what the situation was, and what we were going to do.

I was very struck by that little man at that meeting — he wasn't even the main speaker. The man who spoke most was the provincial of the Jesuits, César Jerez: he had a lot of information because he had a rather close relationship with President Romero's[22] people, and he had secret information about the plans for attacking the church. Monseñor Romero was sitting in a corner, hidden away, insignificant, wearing perhaps his oldest soutane, sitting there with an anxious expression on his face, listening to the testimonies of his priests.

One said: 'I have been accused of setting fire to a field of sugar cane, just because I had a little box of matches in my pocket. You know that I smoke and that I always carry a little box of matches. When the cane caught fire I was nowhere near it, I was in the community celebrating Mass. The catechists themselves are witnesses.' Monseñor sat there just listening. Other priests said: 'Look, this and this is happening to me, Monseñor — the people of ORDEN[23] are about and they are inventing charges against the catechists. We can't meet.' And Monseñor sat there listening, listening.

At the end of the meeting, he said: 'How terrible it is to hear all this.' We were all silent. Monseñor said: 'People are feeling frightened', and I remember his tone of voice. Then he said: 'We haven't got power, we haven't got anything. But we have something greater — we have the truth. We have the gospel, we have the truth, and we are many. We

---

21. Rutilio Grande SJ, who was murdered in March 1977.
22. General Carlos Humberto Romero, president of El Salvador from 1977 until his overthrow in a military coup in 1979.
23. ORDEN — Organización Democrática Nacionalista (Democratic Nationalist Organisation), the government's anti-subversive paramilitary organisation.

are a force that will go on, united, that will stand up to the wave of violence, threats, false testimonies and everything.'

I remember when we left the meeting, we all expected them to be waiting for us. It was such a horrid feeling: the atmosphere outside in the street, the fear that now they were going to fall on us. Monseñor Romero walked along the pavement with his briefcase under his arm — that little man, looking extremely anxious. As we drove into Sonsonate, everyone was silent, there was nothing to say. We had been left with a feeling of 'Take care of yourself if you can.'

The war years
I wasn't able to see Monseñor Romero much after that because my outings alone to San Salvador were restricted. Then I was hastily sent [by the religious order] to Mexico, to get me away from the situation here. I have always had a critical mind, and they might have feared that I would sow my anxieties in the other sisters' heads, and so it was better to transfer me to Mexico. There, it was more difficult for me to follow the situation. I was completely cut off, I felt shut in, and I thought it best to leave. As I say, I had nothing against the sisters — I owe them a lot. But the situation had changed: there were different points of view, and I wanted to be near the church at that time. So I left. I felt a little lost, because I was out of touch with Monseñor. I went straight to my family and my contact with him was limited to listening to his homilies. Of course, I suffered a lot when he was killed.

Before I joined the Sisters of St Clare I wanted to continue working with the people, to be close to them, but without being in a convent. To begin with I was with my father, I wanted to look after my old folks. Eventually I came to work in San Salvador, and the archbishopric gave me work in the four refuges: Domus Mariae, San José de la Montaña, la Basílica and San Roque. From 1981 I worked in the refuge of San Roque, coordinating work there, for five years. The staff had a tough time — occasionally there were selective captures, of the staff as well as of the refugees. It was a very difficult time.

The church during the war

We cannot say that the church as a whole opted to address the problems of the people and their persecution. A part of the church, either because of ignorance or because of its commitment to the dominant classes, tried to stay aloof. In a sense they caused suffering to the church which put itself on the side of the people, and which was more critical of what was happening. Even in the midst of war — and I lived through all the worst times of the war, looking after the refuge, receiving people every week as they arrived, absolutely destroyed, from the war zones — I had a lot of contact with Monseñor Rivera[24] and I always passed on to him news of what was happening. I always said who I was, and he approved and often said: 'I think the only thing for us to do is to be the good Samaritan.' I think that a church more committed to the gospel could have an openness and a fairly critical view, and so draw closer to the people's problems.

After the war

Today, in this time of transition, people's needs are not the same as they were. Throughout the 1980s the church could only respond to the emergency, it was not possible to do anything stable or permanent. Now we can feel the danger of wanting to carry out more routine activities and organise better. We do not hear the prophetic voice when there is no emergency. On top of that, the people themselves are now in a rather different situation where everyone is looking after themselves, having to cope with poverty and unemployment. So the prophetic voice is a little subdued here, too. The factors that motivated us to unite are not there. The prophetic voice seems to be fearful, because the persecution is not over. So I feel there is a danger for the church — even when Monseñor Rivera speaks out, there is

24. Archbishop Arturo Rivera Damas, Archbishop Romero's successor. See page 17.

not much of a supportive echo, so it is a lonely voice. The problem is that everyone is looking out for themselves. It is a little dangerous.

I don't think we were ready to cope with the post-war period. It's as if we didn't think the moment would come when it did. There was nothing planned, it was always a question of emergency, the occasional actions, not a conscious preparation for the role we would play in the post-war period. We haven't had a strong prophetic voice able to unite people. There are only isolated voices.

The forthcoming March elections[25] are hard to predict. I feel the country is in a difficult situation of high unemployment. Whatever president we get won't do anything. Of course, we hope for a government for the majority, but it could also end up like the Guatemalan government, unable to respond to the concerns of the majority. There is a feeling of indifference and hopelessness because of the malice, the lying, of the state. Sixty-two per cent of the people say in the polls that they don't know who they will vote for. That's very sad. Who do the people trust?

Six months later
A letter from Sister Antonia to Pamela Hussey:

> Here things are difficult. The way ahead is not clear. Calderón Sol's government seems to be in cloud-cuckoo land as far as judging the people's aspirations is concerned. He says he is worried about the increase in violence but it is only words, we're getting worse every day. We are awaiting the nominations of the new Supreme Court of Justice. Of course, ARENA wants to control the three powers of the State, but things could change with a good opposition. Let's hope that at least some good heads in the Legislative Assembly can neutralise these

25. The 1994 presidential elections. ARENA candidate Armando Calderón Sol won in the second round, in April, with 68.3 per cent of the vote, so keeping the party in power for a second consecutive term.

dangerous tendencies. They say that 500 men from the National Police are being demobilised because they have said openly that they go in for burglary and kidnapping. They always have done [...]

Things are very obscure now. Threats abound. The death squads are completely free, and impunity calmly reigns. We hope that things will change because God is with his people.

The election campaign

We were in time for the warm-up speeches. This was crude, populist demagogy, beginning with a paean to the party's founder, Roberto D'Aubuisson. Listening, who would have known that the man described in such glowing terms had been notorious for his death squad connections and had been accused by the Truth Commission of ordering the death of Archbishop Romero.

As cries of 'Patria sí, comunismo no' went up from the stage, I felt as if I had fallen into a time trap, and that we were back in the Cold War of the Reagan era. This was very different from the 'reconciliation, reconstruction and prosperity for all', so assiduously cultivated in ARENA television commercials and the speeches of President Cristiani. The topsy-turvy feeling deepened as the discourse moved on to expound on the devastation and death brought by the guerrilla forces. They denounced the amnesty granted to terrorist leaders — no mention of the amnesty for the armed forces — and attacked the Left Coalition's candidate for the presidency, Rubén Zamora, for ordering terrorist killings during the war. Next came the jokes and the stories — the message was the same. The warm-up culminated with the words of a young child: 'No more terrorist killing of children, vote ARENA.'

From Judith Kent, 'ARENA — A party for the people?' in *Central America Report*, May/June 1994.

The novices
Sisters of St Clare, San Antonio Abad

Four novice Sisters of St Clare, aged 21 or 22 and based in the San Antonio Abad community, told us their stories. Because Yolanda, Cruz, Antonia and Reina were only children at the outbreak of the civil war in 1980, their commitment to the revolutionary project was not as strong and clearly articulated as that of the congregation when Pamela visited in 1988.

As children, these young women experienced the hardships of war. Cruz and her family had to leave their town in the department of Cabañas because of what they suffered, and have not returned. Reina experienced the difficulties and dangers of living in a conflict zone, where guerrillas and army frequently clashed and forcible recruitment was common.

Yolanda: What I suffered from most was the tension. Hearing the shooting at night or the plane flying over made me nervous, and there was a time when they were hunting the men to recruit them. I remember that all the men left home at night, leaving only the women. My father used to sleep outside, on the mountain. The soldiers used to pass through, asking for food — and the guerrillas too — but we didn't have any massacres in our canton.

Pamela: What do you think of the church's role in the war situation?

Yolanda: I don't know much about the church because I wasn't very close to it, but some priests were concerned to tell the truth and denounce what was happening. Most of the ones who were killed were killed for that reason. They undertook to tell the people the truth, which it was not possible to broadcast on the radio. For instance, YSAX [the archdiocesan radio station], which reached all the cantons, was cut off many times to prevent people from finding out the truth. The priests gave homilies and brought out bulletins so that the people could learn about the situation — that was why they died. Many catechists also died.

Pamela: Do you see your religious commitment as something that has to do with changes in society and the church — has Christian ministry got anything to do with transforming things?

Cruz: I think religious commitment is great, but you can't change a way of life that exists. It's very difficult for a person to say: 'I'm going to change this or that', if the powerful are in the way. What has to be changed is the mentality of so many young people, adolescents, children, who are beginning their lives — to change their mentality so as to go beyond, to achieve equality. If there is equality it will be possible to change society. As religious, our aim is to help a suffering people out of their suffering and towards this change.

Antonia: Yes, I think there has to be a deep awareness of the meaning of one's commitment: that is, that religious life is not sought only as a refuge, a place of escape. Rather, we are trying to discern more clearly our role in the future of the church and this society.

Pamela: Helped by biblical reflection?

Carmen: When we read the gospels, *Mark* for example, we begin to realise that Jesus was a man who did a lot for the people, who broke many laws that were against life. He fought for life.

Reina: We've had time here for a deeper study of the Bible, learning to appreciate things that Jesus did in his time. Step by step we are learning.

Pamela: What about the question of women's rights? I have heard that religious here concern themselves very little with women's issues.

Antonia: Perhaps it is thought that we should be a more public voice in these matters. But as women in a strongly *macho* church, we have been concerned for some time about our role, our place in the church. So I don't agree with that opinion. Many of us come from homes where we have seen *machismo*, which is not in accordance with the equality created by God. By deepening this concept of the equality of all creation, I think we have been playing our part. Perhaps what is expected is a more public voice, that we speak out more, that our prophetic voice be stronger and more global.

Pamela: What about the question of the priesthood for women?

Antonia: I respect the people who feel called in that way, but I don't think that's what we should be fighting for — a ministry at the same level as the priest. I think we need to discover our role from being women, feminine. God has not discriminated against the feminine. God is a loving God and a feminine God, a mother.

So I would not want a priestly ministry, in order to find my role as a woman. I think there has to be another dimension for us, our femininity has to develop and it has a strong potential, very strong. If men have it one way, we have it another. A woman has a very definite role: she is more determined, more committed. Even under torture, the men were weaker than the women. So there too you can see what we are capable of. It is sad that during the war women played such an important part, and now they are falling back into their old role.

Sister Mark
Sisters of St Clare, Gotera, Morazán

The community in Gotera is made up of Sister Mark, from Northern Ireland, and the only non-Salvadorean, Sisters Elvia and Felipa, and seven young women preparing to be novices. When we met her, Sister Mark had been in Gotera since 1990.

Sister Mark: Sister Anselm Gunn was the first to come here in 1972. The parish has 10 towns and 60 villages — so there was a tremendous amount of work to be done. Soon after, Sister Jean Ryan joined Anselm and they worked together with the priests in the parish. The work was mainly in catechetics: there was a great need for trained people to celebrate the word of God, to instruct others in the faith and to support those who were involved in doing this work. They developed a programme of formation; this grew, as did their work in the parish. In each town and village, there is now a parish team and people prepared to accept the responsibility of celebrating the word, instructing young people in the faith, preparing others to receive the sacraments, and being attentive to the needs of the people.

During the war there was little opportunity for formal education. So the parish became involved in a programme of adult education, trying both to give a basic level of literacy to those involved in catechetics, and to encourage them to pass on what they learned to others. There is also a healthcare programme which is now geared to preventive methods and the use of non-chemical medicines, using plants for medicinal purposes. There is work with women's groups, trying to encourage the women to care for themselves, to achieve a sense of self-esteem, and to take more responsibility for themselves.

Work with young people

Young people are the future of the parish, and in recent years there has been a great development in parish youth work. Training programmes were developed, and there are now 75 youth groups actively working in the parish. The work involves looking at their life, seeing it in the light of the gospel, and relating the gospel to their life, and their life to the gospel. They also look at social situations within the country and internationally, trying to situate their own scene in the wider world. It is interesting to hear the young people speak so fluently about their relationship with God and how the word of God influences their lives. We have used the work of Carlos Mesters[26] as a basis for programmes of study, and this year have been getting the young people to write their own stories: it has been interesting to see some of the work they have done. They are conscious of their cultural background, so we use methods derived from socio-drama and their own culture to assist them in their work with scripture. We are also trying to provide a sound basis for the study of the sacraments, so that they have a good general knowledge of all aspects of the Catholic faith. In recent years there has been a great increase in the number of religious sects in the parish, and they have a large following, so it's important that our people know the foundation of their faith and remain loyal to it.

Marigold: I think it is a pity that so often it is mostly the sects who are giving a lot of attention to young people. What they give them is the feeling of confidence – 'I have made my commitment to the Lord, so now everything is going to be all right' – without any of the formation that you are giving people here.

Mark: Yes, I think you're right and I think that is what the religious sects offer. But I find that our people have a

---

26. Carlos Mesters, a Dutch priest living and working in Brazil (see bibliography). He has played a major part in promoting bible reading among the poor of Latin America.

tremendous sense that God is with them in their journey; they accept both the good and the difficulties in a way that is just marvellous.

God is with them

We were present, for example, when one group returned here after nine years of war-imposed exile in Honduras. They had nothing, no worldly goods. I spoke to one woman who was sitting on a rock; she had three children beside her, was breastfeeding one, and her husband was peeling an orange with a machete. I said to her: 'You know, this must be a very special day for you after all the suffering you have been through.' She said: 'Yes, but God has been with us all the time. He will look after us as he has done in the past.' Another day I spoke to a young boy whose brother had been captured; he was going to try to find him,

---

Evangelical churches

Secular and Catholic critics, most of whom do not seem to have ever stepped foot in an evangelical church to observe for themselves, do not appreciate what draws millions of poor people to join its ranks. This pull includes an intensity of prayer, a simple comprehensible message that seems to make sense out of the surrounding chaos, a moral code that provides guidance (and which in some ways is a throwback to the firm moral code of peasant society), a community in which people call each other brothers and sisters, and a sense of self-respect. Although the evangelical churches are often accused of being foreign imports, at the *barrio* level they may be closer to popular culture than the Catholic church is [...] By virtue of the fact that approximately 15 per cent of the Latin American population finds meaning in evangelical religion, these churches play an important role in society. Even if in their theology they might discourage social activism, their political stance may be evolving.

From Phillip Berryman, 'The Coming of Age of Evangelical Protestantism' in *LADOC*, November/December 1994.

---

to discover if he was still alive, or what had happened to him. I again said: 'This is very difficult for you.' His mother is an invalid and the older brother who was captured had looked after her. The boy said: 'I'm confident that God will take care of us.' This, to me, is the living faith that Christ spoke of and recognised among the people in his day. The miracles happen because the people have faith.

Another day I stood at the graveside of a young woman who had just died having given birth to a son three weeks previously. The official mourners chanted the lament as the neighbours struggled in the heat of the midday sun to fill the grave with the clay that had hardened from the rain of the day before. A drunk worked feverishly, dancing on the clay that already filled the hole. 'Look,' he said, 'she never failed to give me a *tortilla*. I won't spare her my effort now. She was a great woman. I won't spare her my effort.'

Pamela: It sounds as if the young women come to you because they appreciate the work you do among the people.

Mark: That is partly correct, but I would also say they have come because of the desire, firmly planted within each of them, to follow God in a way that is special, and they see the Sisters of St Clare as providing a way of life that is attractive to them.

Here in Gotera at the moment there are 10 of us. I'm the only foreigner. Elvia has made her final profession, and Felipa is hoping to make hers at the end of this year. We also have seven postulants [pre-novitiate stage]. This year we are celebrating the 800th anniversary of the birth of St Clare, and we feel that she has shone her light on us here in El Salvador. We are grateful to God for the blessing of these young women who have come in search of him and to serve the people.

Pamela: So their primary commitment is to follow Christ?

Mark: Definitely.

Pamela: When I was here a few years ago, the young Salvadorean sisters here were obviously committed to the struggle, the cause of the people. I remember thinking: 'I wonder, when this war is over, if their commitment to religious life is going to be as strong; because it seems it is almost inextricably bound up at the moment with commitment to the revolutionary cause.' In the event, several of the young women who were with you during the war left, perhaps because the religious life and the struggle were too bound up with each other. The numbers you have now indicate that the religious life — for these young women at any rate — stands on its own, so to speak, although of course it includes commitment to the building of a more just society.

Mark: These seven young people have come after the war, with clear knowledge of our way of life. Most of them have had the opportunity to take part in our programme of candidacy, where they spent one day a month with us for one or two years, and took part in retreats and had the opportunity to live with us for one to three weeks. So they have seen and know our way of life. They too feel called to centre their lives on God and the word of Christ and to put this into practice in their lives through service of the people. I think it's increasingly evident to them that to serve the people is not enough. But to spend one's entire day in the chapel is not what is being asked of them either. Contemplation in action is what has attracted them. Our way of life is contemplative, but this contemplation bears fruit in our action and involvement with the people. Conversely, our involvement with the people through our pastoral work and the encounters we have with them, enriches our prayer life.

A new way of being a sister
The Little Community

Sister Noemí belongs to La Pequeña Comunidad, the Little Community, a small group of Sisters whose bravery during the conflict saved many lives. She now leads the pastoral team based in the returned refugee community of Nueva Esperanza, in the coastal area of Usulután.

Marigold: Noemí, you are soon going to celebrate 23 years in religious life. Will you tell me something of how you began?

Noemi: A significant date for me is 16 November, doubly so now because it is the anniversary of the murder of the Jesuit priests [see note 19, page 32] — several of them were friends of mine — and the two women. It was on 16 November 1971 that I embarked on the experience of religious life with the sisters of the Little Community, three of whom had started on 9 December 1970. At that time we didn't have a name, we were a group of young women who wanted to live a life consecrated to God and at the service of the poor. We met without any name and without any pretensions. We wanted to serve God by working towards the formation of the base ecclesial communities, which in those years were influenced by Vatican II and more concretely by Medellín. The BEC was something new in the work of building the church.

Marigold: What attracted you to this form of religious life rather than the more traditional form?

Noemí: I come from a Catholic family and I think I owe a lot to my grandmother. My parents brought me up in the faith, but my grandmother's influence was greater, I think.

55

At that time Monseñor Romero was the parish priest of the cathedral in San Miguel, and my grandmother took my older sister and me to all the Masses, the processions, and so on.

My experience of the base ecclesial communities was from the clinic which a religious congregation ran as a form of social work. That was where I met the other three sisters. They were aspirants, preparing to be novices in a religious congregation where one was the seamstress. I was there because I wanted to be a religious, and a priest had advised me to get to know the sisters, to see if this was my path — to see how they lived, how they worked. At that time I was working in the clinic as a secretary and I spoke to the director, telling her of my concerns. Then they invited me to attend all the formation of the aspirants.

So it was that I took part in their formation. A Belgian priest, Father Peter, arrived. He had only just arrived in the country and he asked if he could give lessons to the aspirants, so as to learn the language. He celebrated the Eucharist. So I began to study.

For me it was like discovering a new concept of the church and religious life. I can say that with hindsight; at the time, it was like an awakening for me, it was all new and wonderful. I would like to be like that now. These other young women were going to enter the novitiate, but just at the moment of entering it they said: 'This isn't the right path for us. We come from poor peasant families.'

Although the congregation ran this clinic for the poor, they were mainly dedicated to the education of the upper classes. We asked ourselves: 'How are we, coming from poor families, going to prepare ourselves to educate the children of the rich?' This life seemed to be fairly meaningless, and we felt more drawn to issues of justice and peace. We began to study the documents of the church and to sense the renewal in the church: the Medellín documents greatly inspired us. The time came when we felt we had to work in the communities — we didn't call them base ecclesial communities to begin with, we called them

Christian groups, *ecclesiolas*. Father Peter was working with the communities at that time; he invited me and I began to take part in a group.

Of course, I was 18 or 19 then, and taking part in an adult group; I was an extremely shy person, and there was a very fat woman in the group, and I used to hide behind her so that I shouldn't be asked a question. It was a new experience: we didn't meet to pray but to talk about life and its problems. That woke me up, and in spite of my shyness I began to be part of the group and discovered my Christian vocation more clearly.

Then began a greater understanding of the church, of what it meant to be a Christian. I started to work in the communities, and we came to feel that the mother of the experience of the Little Community — the people called us the Little Community, we didn't look for a name — was precisely the base ecclesial community, which had given us an experience of consecrated life outside a religious institution. So we went on from there.

When we began the Little Community we had to work to keep ourselves financially, and we had to go on studying because we hadn't finished our studies. So we spent our free time at weekends working with the communities. We didn't want to be economically dependent on our parents or anyone else, we wanted to learn to live by ourselves.

Committing our lives to the community

Then the moment came when we wanted to express our commitment. The four of us began to reflect on what this meant, because members of religious congregations take their evangelical vows before a superior. We had no superior, but we wanted to make the commitment. Normally in a congregation you make a commitment for one year, and then renew it, and I remember that at that moment, in our youthful courage, we asked ourselves: 'How are we going to commit ourselves for one year?' If I had got married, I wouldn't have married a man for just one year, and then said: 'I'll see whether I stay with you or not.' I thought it was a commitment for life, and we reflected together that our commitment was to be for ever. So we did it.

We took a risk, but up to now, we have managed it. I don't feel that I have wasted my time. On the contrary I feel that this experience has given meaning to my life. It has filled my life and I feel happy — after 23 years I can say I am happy that God has chosen me for this way. And I still have the same dreams.

The effects of the war

We suffered persecution during the conflict. Our house was searched and we had to move every six months. I was captured a number of times. Even after the offensive, after the accords, we had problems: threats, anonymous messages, telephone calls. But I feel that all this was an experience that enriched us. One of our sisters [Silvia Arriola, see page 61] is counted among the martyrs of the people.

When we made our commitment we said we wanted to become incarnate in the life of the people. We used to say: 'How can we do that, since we are the people?' But that was how it was, and at that historic moment we felt that God was demanding of us that we live the process we were experiencing, that we weren't going to live our Christian life outside the historical context of the time. So it was that the people we worked with in the BECs became conscientised, evangelisation led us to make a commitment in history, and all our people were committing themselves to the transformation of society: if they lived in a slum, they joined a slum organisation to change the situation there; if they lived in the countryside, they joined a rural organisation that was fighting for the peasants' demands. Workers, teachers, students — all our people were committing themselves from the gospel to the transformation of society.

When the first offensive happened, on 10 January 1980, we realised that the most difficult time was about to begin. We were asked if, as consecrated women, we could accompany pastorally all these people who were involved in this movement of transformation. So we reflected, and we heard the voice of God in this request. Because of the situation, priests and religious had to abandon some places inside the war zones, but we couldn't go back on our commitment, we had to stay inside. So two of us went to the war zones to accompany these people pastorally. One of the sisters, Silvia Arriola, was killed with 97 others in the town of Cutumán Camones in the department of Santa Ana, in the west of our country.

We felt that this persecution confirmed our experience because now our Little Community is marked by martyrdom, just like other families: here in our country there isn't a family without its dead, its captured, its kidnapped.

'A time of saints'

Archbishop Chávez was one of those who opened up possibilities for the transformation of the Salvadorean church. Monseñor Chávez was a very intuitive man and, as I see it, he prepared the ground for an evangelisation that bore fruit with the message of Monseñor Romero. Monseñor Romero brought to flower the seed that had been sown in the time of Monseñor Chávez. Monseñor Romero was like the rain on the ground — one understands so much more when one has lived in the country and learnt a peasant's language and the importance of the rain for his little crop. So the seed was able to grow and give fruit a hundredfold. Monseñor Romero gave the bishops credibility, but Monseñor Chávez had already helped us to believe in the role of the pastor.

I think the period of Monseñor Romero was one of the best moments of the Salvadorean church, because we lived through everything: prophecy, martyrdom, a time of saints. Monseñor Romero was a real saint, like men and women we have known who have walked with us, who have given a testimony of fidelity to Jesus while living our history. Being a Christian among the Salvadorean people in these times has not been easy. It has been a question of taking on history and committing oneself. It was thanks to a pastor like Monseñor Romero that this was possible.

The Little Community

Marigold: And the Little Community — was it linked to any congregation or was it independent?

Noemí: It was totally independent. We began in the days of Monseñor Chávez, and I remember that Father Peter went to tell him that he had seen the beginning of this experience, and that we were all young women of only 19 or 20. Monseñor Chávez said to Father Peter: 'Leave it — if this is of God it will endure; if it is not, it will die.' Now, after 24 years, we think it is of God, because we have been able to walk in an experience that God called us into, through no merit of our own. God has intervened in our lives, and we have been his instrument.

Marigold: And you felt the need to be independent because you didn't believe you would be able to work as you wanted within any of the congregations?

Noemí: At that time we were not very inspired by the religious life as we saw it. It was 1969, 1970, and we saw people anxious to do something, but prevented by the institution from offering a greater service to the poor. We began to think that there would be a limit on the services we could offer, and so we wanted to be independent of such institutional links. We were inspired by the life of Mary in Nazareth, Mary in the midst of the people. But at that time we didn't want to belong to an institution because we saw that it limited the service to the poor — I couldn't say the same thing now. We also noted that during wartime in our country there were many religious men and women who wanted to do something, and were prevented by their institution. The contribution that many people could offer was limited and clandestine.

We have no organisational link — although this doesn't mean that we are not in communion, in touch — of course we are. Our presence here is authorised by the bishop. He knows about our experience. We think the Little Community may continue, but we also feel a time may come when God will ask the opposite of us. We want to stay faithful to the intuition of the Spirit at this time.

Vows of Silvia Arriola

Sister Silvia Arriola of the Little Community pronounced these vows in the presence of the base Christian communities and Archbishop Romero. Silvia was murdered on 18 January 1981.

In a society whose ideals are power, possession and pleasure, I pray that I may be a sign of what it really means to love. I will do my best to be a sign that Christ Jesus alone is Lord of history — that he is present here in our midst — and that he is capable of inspiring a love mightier than our own instincts, mightier than all of the economic and political forces, mightier than death itself. My one desire is to lead a life in the following of Christ — he who was poor, chaste, and obedient to the will of his Father. I wish to live for him alone and his saving work, as his disciple.

I promise our Lord that I will be faithful — in sickness and in health, in youth and old age, in tranquillity and persecution, in joy and sorrow. I promise to do my best to share in his incarnation among the poorest of the poor, and to imitate his poverty and solidarity with them in their liberation struggle.

This is my hope and desire: to share in his evangelising mission among human beings, concentrating all the power of my will and affections on him and on all my sisters and brothers, and living in continual quest of the Father's will: in his word, in the church, in the signs of the times, and in the poor.

From Hussey, 1989, *op cit.*

A new way of praying
A 'pray-in' at San Antonio Abad

One evening Sister Jean Ryan and Pamela Hussey attended a *rezo*, a prayer service led by an official *rezadora*, a prayer lady, for Niña Paquita, who had just died. This is an established ceremony in poor communities, in which the prayer lady follows a set pattern of readings and prayers. The difference in this one was that after the bible readings there were spontaneous commentaries from those present, most of whom were members of the local base ecclesial community. Their contributions showed both understanding of the text and an ability to relate it to everyday life. One woman said: 'The Bible is my examination of conscience.'

The living room of the house was packed with people sitting in rows facing a small altar decorated with pictures and flowers. A photograph of Monseñor Romero and a poster celebrating the 800th anniversary of the birth of St Clare adorned the walls. The pray-in was clearly a social occasion as well as a way of expressing the community's sympathy to the family of Niña Paquita, and the prayers were followed by cold drinks and cakes.

Rosy's school of prayer

One morning Nelly del Cid (see page 20) took us to meet Rosy, a *rezadora* living in the marginalised community of Colonia San Rafael. Rosy explained to us her thoughts on prayer and how she helps women's groups to pray.

Rosy: What I want is for everyone to understand the meaning of the things they are going to do. One way to help people to participate is to motivate them: they need to feel that they, as women, are being called to meet Christ. One way of doing that is when we pray the rosary. We say the Our Father and the five mysteries, but before that we read

the Bible, and consider the circumstances of our country
and how we are living now. Then we find the right reading
and we explain it within the group. We explain it as if we
are taking the grains of corn off the cob. People ask: 'What
does this mean?' Sometimes I don't have the answers, so I
look at my friend Nelly. She has been learning with the
people. There are questions that I ask, or that she asks.
When I don't know, I look at her, because she knows more
about religion than I do. There are things I am still asking
myself, and I don't know the answers. Perhaps it is a
question of time and I will know more in the future.

I always work with the same people — that's my style. I
used not to like praying. Now I feel that I am doing things
as well as I can. I don't know how people see me, if they
think I am doing right things or wrong ones. I do things as
I learned to do them. I needed to do things in this way
because, at first, I didn't like to pray. People tried to teach
me but I wasn't interested. But circumstances change [...]
people look to me now. People want to keep things as they
were before, but they seldom live in the present and see the
things that are happening around us.

I like people to know why they are praying. What is the
point of praying, without a sense of what they are doing?
Sometimes they pray just for something to do, without any
understanding. Sometimes they are even too embarrassed
to pray. This is what I am trying to change, but it is difficult.
We need to keep going. Sometimes I say to someone: 'Look,
pray the Our Father', and the person says: 'But I am
embarrassed if someone asks me.' And I say: 'Don't be
afraid. If you need to pray you will not be embarrassed.'

Praying our own prayers

Once we went to Apopa and we met a lady whose son had
had an accident. Nobody wanted to pray, but some people
said: 'If there are no prayers he will not be saved.' The lady
asked: 'Can you pray the rosary for the dead?' People think
that prayers will save the person — but what is she getting
from her own prayers? I don't understand it. The lady was

63

very worried and I felt sorry for her, but I had never prayed in public before. She asked me to do it as a favour for her. I told people that I had never prayed before. But then, what have they taught me? Every day we must say the Our Father and the Hail Mary and other prayers before we go to sleep — but they don't teach us the most important prayers of all, which is our own prayers.

The lady from Apopa told me: 'Child, read the prayers.' I felt sorry for her and I couldn't say no. Nobody wanted to pray or even to read a prayer. So I took the Bible and I found a reading there. I said: 'Why are they saying Hail Mary without understanding it? This is not good.' They pray to impress others, but without understanding.

Prayer parties

I am trying to change these things, but it is difficult. Sometimes you find people who think in a different way. They don't accept what I am trying to tell them. This is why I tried to learn to play the guitar: people like parties and they feel motivated by the music.

People see others gathering and they are curious. I am interested in these people. I say: 'You, come here please and pray the Our Father.' They refuse because they are scared. They haven't been taught. I then ask five people to pray the Hail Mary and between us we pray the whole rosary. We sing songs between the mysteries. A song, a line or two, and another mystery. We explain things and make things known. To think that I didn't like to pray!

Women learning to stand on their own
The archdiocesan women's programme

Gloria Guzmán was the head of the archdiocesan women's programme. Before she began this work Gloria had belonged, with her family, to a Christian base community in San Francisco Mejicanos, a parish in the capital. It was there that she began working with women. Our conversations took place at a meeting with a women's group.

Gloria: Luckily for us, we were working with a priest — a feminist priest — who had some interesting views on the situation of women.

We organised our first workshop in the rural zone of the department of La Libertad, and invited the wives of the delegates of the word, all of whom were men. It was a big parish with 59 male celebrants — and one female. Thirty wives came to the workshop.

We had no experience of developing formation programmes for women and we didn't know how they would turn out, but we were personally concerned that our situation had to change, especially in the church, where it is sometimes more difficult. Women from the different cantons came to the parish centre for the two day workshop. This was an achievement in itself, because it meant leaving the small children and not seeing to meals.

The programme had five themes, relating women to work, health, the family, church, and the organisation. Many of the women, as is normal in our country, have been brought up to be shadows of someone else — we can only function in that way. For example when we talked about women and the family, we touched on the theme of men's physical violence against women, and we asked: 'Do you think this is right, that the man should beat his wife?' And some of them said — I will never forget it — some of them said: 'If she gives him cause, yes, it's right.' The women themselves were accepting a situation of violence.

Working with this group of women we became aware that we had to begin with questions closer to their lives, not so much about our own positions. We had taken some small steps and reached some conclusions, but it could not be a question of our saying: 'This is right, and this is not.'

For the next workshop we asked the women who took part in the first workshop to invite their neighbours. At that time we had no plan for the number of workshops we wanted to do, or what we hoped to get out of them. We were more concerned to try out this system. So the next group was not made up of wives of the celebrants of the word but of their neighbours, and it was a much more active group.

The parish priest and I were very struck by the fact that the celebrant of the word, who is in some sense a 'little priest' in the community, often overshadows the women when it should be the other way round. The women who came to the second workshop did not have husbands who were so active in the church, and they could participate more fully. Very often the celebrants of the word, because they are literacy teachers, health promoters and a number of other things, have to be away from home a great deal. Their wives therefore have to stay at home more, to look after the children and the fields. So it would seem that the celebrant of the word was able to develop at the cost of having someone at home who would take care of all the domestic tasks. This was an evaluation we made after that second workshop.

Forming the women's programme

At that time, in 1986 and 1987, there were not many women's programmes in the parishes. Then we began to be interested in the archdiocesan programme for widows and orphans. At an early stage of this programme, economic support was given monthly for one or two years, channelled through the parishes. The parishes eventually said there were other women who were not widows but whose situation was the same and who received no help. We began to try to change the concept of the programme of support for widows and orphans.

In 1989 the women's programme was formed, no longer a programme in support of widows and orphans, victims of the war, but a programme for the promotion of women, with priority given to war widows and orphans. We began to experiment – with great difficulty – because the archdiocese had never before made it a priority to focus on women. It had been a programme for widows and orphans, so a programme solely for women was questioned. Since 1993, however, the programme has been more stable — although there are still some difficulties.

Training pastoral agents

Since 1993, we have run what we call the School for the Promotion of Pastoral Agents, specialising in women's issues. We began a series of workshops which we hope will go on until the end of this year, 1994. Last year we held 10 workshops of three days each.

My colleague Claudia and I, who have been coordinating these workshops, have learnt a lot. We have an integral theme, the theme of gender which affects women more directly than men but which we never talk about in ordinary life. The theme of doctrine, as we call it, deals with themes more specifically related to the church and the Bible. The other part is the methodological aspect: if we are going through a process it is important to know how we are doing this. It is not only a question of content, but of how we can go on teaching and learning.

Claudia: As Gloria said, it was the first time that a systematic training process had been initiated. Until 1992 there had been only occasional workshops for women in the parishes. But in 1993 the school was founded so that pastoral agents specialising in the promotion of women could work at the parish level. A training programme was designed for two years, 1993 and 1994, with the content Gloria has mentioned. By the end of that time the women were to be able to initiate an organisational and educational process in their parishes, in their communities, with different groups of women: they would be agents charged with the multiplication of the experience at local level. The women present here were the pioneers in this task. This year a new group will begin which will end its training at the end of 1995. It is a three year process in practice, two of training and one of follow-up at local level.

Pamela: What problems do you come up against? I imagine it is difficult for the men to accept that the women can organise and talk.

Gloria: I said before that within the institution it has been difficult to carry out a programme like this; for me this is one of the principal problems. The problems come mostly from men, but there are also women who do not share the vision of this kind of process. All the obstacles that have been put in the way of the programme reflect our patriarchal, *macho* society. It is one thing to criticise constructively, but often criticisms have been made in a destructive spirit. It is basically fear of change, because this is not a simple health programme, it is a programme that looks at us as women and at our partners as men. Above all, it requires a major change on the part of the men, because it means a loss of many privileges that they have always had. Faced with this, they come up with any number of obstacles.

In spite of that, there are compensations: we are lucky to have an auxiliary bishop who supports this kind of work. At national level there is no other bishop who would consider this work important, as Monseñor Rosa Chávez has done over the last years. For us it is very gratifying, and it is valuable in the sense that in the hierarchical Catholic church, the words of a bishop, a priest or a sister have great influence, while those of lay people are not so valued. In that church structure, having the support of someone like

Monseñor Rosa Chávez compensates for all our other internal and institutional problems.

Another difficulty is that there are many tasks at institutional level which take up administrative time. We often haven't got the time to prepare a workshop well, or read a book that we ought to read, or take part in other training processes to nourish our practice. In this country we live in a state of stress which wears us down, but we have to cope with it.

Pamela: What role are women religious playing in this?

Gloria: Considering the number of religious in this country, there are not many involved. You don't feel that the religious are making proposals or that they want women to be ordained. There are some religious saying this, but I don't think this path has been well trodden. Some non-Salvadorean religious are expressing the need — but on the other hand there is criticism of the priesthood, because it is nearly always the priest who decides what has to be done. In many parishes we don't yet have a democratic way of carrying out pastoral work, and part of the feminist movement wants change in the concept of work and working methods. My opinion is that it is important that women should be ordained. These are significant changes for women and we have a lot to do in the church.

Margarita: There are some religious who help us, and we were able to get together a group of 10 women after we had had a workshop, but the men always put obstacles in the way. When we gave the invitation the man was always the first to answer, refusing either on account of the children, or because she had to be at home, or because we were going to liberate them. I said this was not about liberation, but about the dignity of the women. Dignity is greater than liberation, I said, because liberation can take wrong roads too. But the men don't think of the dignity of the woman, of making her aware of her worth; they think that she will have more power than they do. They are wrong. There are women who think like that too, who say that this won't help them.

We have continued working with the group, which is now down to about eight women. It isn't a stable group but we will go on working and fighting. The neighbourhood is quite big but few women come. They always have an excuse — that their husband doesn't let them, or that they can't bring the children. I tell them that they can bring them, it isn't for long, just one or two hours. We hope this will grow. We have the opportunity in the parish — some religious sisters have come this year who have already taken part, and the parish priest supports all the pastoral work.

María Elena: I didn't know anything about base communities until last year, when they invited us to a day when Monseñor [Rivera Damas] was going to the Fourth Conference [in Santo Domingo] and he wanted to take discussion material with him. It was the first time that I had taken part at church level. So when the opportunity came to take part in this school, I liked the idea very much. I have always been involved in work for women and I see it as necessary for one to go on discovering things that have been hidden inside oneself, both to be able to help others and to form oneself, as a liberated woman.

After that year in the school I began [carrying out pastoral work] in the parish with another woman. We don't do too much because it isn't looked on kindly by the women's husbands, who have begun to think that we want to change the women so that they will rule things in the house. But the parish priest and the parish council support us so that we can work with groups.

The parochial academy is at our disposal, we have made our training plan, and there are 38 or 40 women. Each one of us has our own small group of women, but we have a meeting day when we speak specifically on the theme of women and above all we try to pass on to them what we learn in the school. We take advantage of every opportunity to speak on the theme of women: for example, in the rosary, or any other religious meeting, we focus on the Virgin as the special woman. Then there are problems — even the men in the community have told us that we are feminists. This has come as a shock and is something that we haven't been able to explain very clearly: we need to.

Angela: Through the training workshops provided by the women's programme we have discovered that we have to live our faith and value ourselves as women. We have seen that *machismo* means that a woman has no freedom — she is enslaved to serve in the house, she must look after the children and have everything ready when the man comes home, and that the work she does in the house is not valued. We have understood this through the workshops and our experiences. I found the dialogue with other women good because, before, I thought that I had the biggest problems.

All this has made us think that as women we have work to do and we must carry on together in this process. The meeting of couples, women and men, has to motivate us too. We must use a method where the men can see that they have equal rights with the women, and the women with the men. It is an area where the couple face a great commitment and challenge before God, the family and society.

Rufina Amaya
Ciudad Segundo Montes

We set out early one morning for Ciudad Segundo Montes (Segundo Montes City) in Morazán, which took its name in memory of one of the six Jesuits murdered in November 1989. It was repopulated in 1989 by 8,600 people who returned from the Colomoncagua refugee camp in Honduras, where they had spent nine years. An extraordinary degree of organisation and production had been achieved in Colomoncagua — Father Segundo Montes, reporting on his first visit there, said it had turned upside down all his theories on development — and this was transported back to the barren and deserted fields and hills of Morazán, where the returned refugees began the difficult task of resettling and making a living in a country still at war.

Rufina Amaya was the only survivor of the massacre by the military of the whole population of the village of Mozote in 1981. The 1993 report of the truth commission set up under the terms of the peace accords, describes the event thus:

> On December 10, 1981, in the hamlet of El Mozote, department of Morazán, all the men, women and children who were in that place were taken unresistingly by units of the Atlacatl battalion. After spending the night shut up in the houses, on the following day, 11 December, they were deliberately and systematically executed, by groups. First the men were tortured and executed, then the women were executed, and finally the children, in the places where they were shut up. The number of identified victims exceeded 200. The figure increases if the unidentified victims are taken into account.[27]

27. Truth Commission report, *De la Locura a la Esperanza*. San Salvador/ New York: United Nations, 1993.

The entire edition of *The New Yorker* of 6 December 1993 was devoted to an article by Mark Danner, 'The Massacre at El Mozote'. It describes the meeting with Rufina of some members of the Argentine team investigating the slaughter:

> At the black road, the Argentines turned left, as they did each evening, heading down to Gotera, but this time they stopped in front of a small house — a hut, really, made of scrap wood and sheet metal and set among banana trees some 15 yards from the road. Getting out of the car, they climbed through the barbed wire and called out, and soon there appeared at the door a middle-aged woman, heavyset, with high cheekbones, strong features, and a powerful air of dignity.

When the Argentines told her of the skulls they had found that day — 25 of them, all but two the skulls of children — Rufina said: 'Didn't I tell you? All you could hear was that enormous screaming.'

Rufina got away to the refugee camp in Colomoncagua, Honduras, and now lives in Ciudad Segundo Montes. We sat with her in her hut and heard her reflections on life after the war, while her small daughter carefully brushed and braided her mother's hair.

Rufina Amaya: At this moment we women need to have spiritual and moral strength to face up to all the problems of our situation in every country. Because this is happening in all countries: women have always been devalued in every aspect and it is not right that that should be so. As women we have to recover our values, our rights and our dignity in order to be equal to men, to have the same strength, and for men to recognise that. We are all human and we all have to be equal. God did not make some of us more and some of us less. Here, we women in the church are always working with women's groups, which we call Congregations of Christian Mothers for Peace, on behalf of the pastoral team of Morazán and also of San Salvador. And this makes us think and reflect on some bible readings where it is clear that women were the bravest. They went to look in the tomb. They were brave enough to go there when the men did not have enough courage. So why should we stand by and see women's human rights being violated in all sorts of ways?

Now that we women have managed to speak out a little bit about the role of women, we think that what the constitutions of El Salvador and other countries say about women having equal rights is real. We don't mean that we ought to have more than the men; no, never, but we ought to have a dialogue. The first thing for us in defending our rights is to know how to defend them and how to respect them. Because, if we can defend our rights through dialogue, we won't fight, we'll begin to talk, to reflect as women and with our husbands, what will be the best future for our children, for our family.

The truth is that the best health, the best life, the best future is to live in peace with our family. If we can begin to overcome the problems in the home and live together as a Christian family, then we'll be able to live together as a community and give our children a Christian education which serves as an example. The Catholic church recognises that men have been valued above women. The church's concern is that there should be love for all. This God we truly love and who loves us all should be a light for a family and for a people. If we don't really believe that we are all human beings and have that living faith in our hearts, perhaps we won't be able to live in peace. Because peace will come when we all realise that we are brothers and sisters, children of the same father. Not of the same mother, but yes of the same father.

The word of God which we take into our hearts, the living faith in God, is the greatest treasure we can have. No one can take that away and, really, that is what is needed in our people. Some of us believe, others don't. Some think only of power and money and whoever has them gives the

> The New Evangelisation makes it indispensable for the church in our continent to face up to the challenge of making a qualitative leap inside and outside herself: to be a decided and active promoter of the dignity of women. True to her origins, the church must become a true sign of communion and also of participation between men and women, joyfully receiving the charisms which each has received from the one Spirit.
>
> From 'Woman in the Church and in Latin American Culture',
> the contribution of Latin American women to
> the Fourth Conference of Latin American Bishops, Santo Domingo, 1992.

orders. And that is a mistake — to feel that if he's got money then he has a lot of power and wants to be greater than God. There is nobody greater than God. The big mistake people make is about money. If someone has enough money he no longer cares if his brother is in the street or another brother has fallen down, he doesn't help him up. Why? Because he has what he needs to live and the life of others doesn't matter to him. And the important thing is to love your brother as yourself. That is the commandment of the word of God. We may have everything, but if we don't see our brother, we are losing the best thing.

It is pitiful to see that a country like yours which is so rich and developed still has people living on the streets with nowhere to sleep. It is painful because, in a developed country the responsibility lies with the government to look after the people, if the government is humane. El Salvador is not a developed country, it is a poor country. But its economic resources have been badly used. That's why there is so much poverty and that's what caused the war, because there has been bad distribution of the riches of the country. El Salvador could produce enough for everyone, but the distribution has been manipulated by the rich.

Pamela: Do you think the Salvadorean people feel deceived because things have not changed much since the end of the conflict?

75

Rufina: There is a lot of concern. For the majority of the poor the concern is to see changes after so much suffering — yet we are pretty much the same as before. Government policy has hardly changed, nor has the economic situation. There are poor people still living in places where it is really not possible to live. We have come out of a war and so much suffering and loss of loved ones and we see that we still cannot have a true and just peace in our country because the accords which were made are not complied with. The demand of all the citizens of El Salvador now is that the accords be fulfilled so that peace will last.

Marigold: Can you tell us more about the organisation of women?

Rufina: In Segundo Montes the organisation of women is quite strong. There are two groupings: the Congregations of Mothers for Peace and the Association of Women, although it is often the same women in both. The Congregations are purely Christian. We have monthly assemblies, sometimes of 60 to 80 women. When we get out good advance publicity we get more.

Pamela: Is awareness of women's rights growing?

Rufina: Yes. We've always explained our rights to the large number of women who come to the Congregations of Mothers and in our pastoral work. Many women are beginning to understand and to demand that their dignity be respected, because if we don't talk about the rights of women and the dignity of women, we ourselves are violating women's rights.

Marigold: Can everyone here in Segundo Montes earn a living?

Rufina: No. Only a few have jobs. The majority are wondering how to live, with their little plots, growing a few basic things. Some go outside the community to work as labourers, for example, because there are not enough jobs in Segundo Montes.

My job is social work. It has no salary. We live with a little allowance that they give as an encouragement — not a salary, just a minimum for expenses such as transport and the odd meal. But it is not a salary like the other workers get. My commitment has always been to God. In Honduras I organised the Congregation of Mothers, and my commitment has always been to the word of God. I can't stop that just because they don't give me a salary, and while I can I shall keep up the effort to work with the mothers.

Marigold: Have you any hope for the future?

Rufina: Yes, my hope is that now that we are here in peace, the country will remain at peace. We have faith and hope that we shall live better, even if it is only that minimum of us who are working. And I have hope for the future of my daughter too, God willing, if we have peace.

Pamela: Have you any message for us to take home with us?

Rufina: The message I would give to the women of your country is to tell them to carry on, to recover their rights as human beings, that the rights of all human beings are equal. Men must understand that we all have the same rights and the same duties in all countries. We must struggle for respect for the rights and dignity of women, but if we want our rights respected, we ourselves must respect the rights of others. That is how one builds, by respecting and loving and by being respected and loved. That is what is needed at this moment in order for us to become examples among our people and not stay with our arms folded.

We have to study, we have to read the Bible and look for what spaces are available for women in the Bible, beginning above all with our mother, the most holy Mary.

She was the mother of Christ. What were the steps Mary took on behalf of her son? She was a committed woman, who saw her son and who struggled, and she too was converted. We women must keep that as an example so that we can convert ourselves like Mary. She didn't betray Jesus, she didn't betray God. We too must be a fortress because we are human beings and although we are weak, God will help us in our weakness and protect us. That is what I would say.

Sandra, in Perquín
The subversive memory of the people

The Museum of the Revolution: Homage to the Heroes and Martyrs, in Perquín, Morazán, enshrines the act of re-membering, putting together what has been dis-membered, preserving the people's history. The women in Suchitoto witnessed to this need to remember by retelling their stories; Suyapa in Chalatenango (see page 127) is working to ensure that their history is passed on intact to the next generation.

It is significant that the desire to capture and enshrine memory in a museum came from a group of women ex-combatants, of whom Sandra was one. We met her towards the end of our day in Morazán, an astonishingly youthful-looking woman considering what she had been through in the war years.

Standing outside the museum in the town of Perquín, a town which had been at the centre of the zone controlled by the FMLN during the conflict, she told us of its beginnings.

Sandra: The initiative for the museum came from women ex-combatants, and it coincided with the ideas of PADECOMSM [Council for the Development of the Communities of Morazán and San Miguel] and CEBES [Base Ecclesial Communities of El Salvador]. So we began to move as a community and on 31 December 1992, with the signing of the peace accords, we founded the Museum of the Revolution. One of the aims is to leave something which will give the story of the experience we have lived through, especially of those who died to build something better for El Salvador. We need to know how to value the experience, here and now and in the future. It mustn't be wiped from our memories.

A nation's memory

In Chile during the military dictatorship of 1973-89, women weavers known as *arpilleristas* used appliqué tapestries to record the history of that time, and the names of their loved ones who disappeared under the regime of General Augusto Pinochet. They have been called 'the repositories of the nation's memory, which is essentially feminine'.

In Moscow there is a Cemetery of the Fallen Idols, a post-*glasnost* and post-*perestroika* park, in which large statues of Stalin and other notorious leaders of the Soviet regime have been collected, defaced and deliberately smashed. Children climb all over them. A Russian guide tells tourists: 'We must not forget. They must know what happened.'

In Guatemala the bishops have set up an interdiocesan project called Recovery of the Historical Memory. They will collect testimonies from witnesses of 35 years of armed violence and publish the results in the hope that knowing the truth will be an important step towards forgiveness, reconciliation and peace.

Museum of the Revolution

Sandra spoke of the special importance of educating the children through workshops, the painting of murals, and similar projects. The celebrations of the first anniversary of the peace accords were dedicated to the children of Morazán, and a special commemoration was made of the many children killed in the war.

The museum had had a lot of publicity and many visitors, which was remarkable considering that it is much further to the north of the Torola river than many people would usually venture. 'Excursions come from different parts of the country,' Sandra told us, 'from the universities and so on, and people have expressed great interest in learning about the experience, especially people from the cities who didn't see the war so close to them, and now want to understand it.'

We were taken through the rooms of the museum, some lined with photos of the heroes and martyrs, going back in history to Emiliano Zapata from Mexico (whose name was adopted by the leaders of the 1994 Zapatista uprising), Farabundo Martí of the 1932 uprising in El Salvador, and including well-known figures of the recent civil war. One fascinating display showed the battered equipment used by *Radio Venceremos*, the FMLN radio station which broadcast throughout the conflict.

Trenches had been preserved outside, since this was a conflict zone, and the small 'tents' for sleeping, simple bits of plastic placed over a low frame, just enough for one person to crawl into. A bomb crater dated from 1981. We were told that Mass used to be celebrated in the open air. 'Many of the guerrillas were committed Christians, and the church played an important part in the war. It didn't encourage the armed struggle, but church people worked to raise people's consciousness of the reasons for the struggle and the need for change.'

Women after the war

Pamela: Sandra, what about the women like you who did so much during the war, who showed themselves capable of carrying out such a wide variety of tasks, are they going to be able to continue developing their skills and using their gifts?

Sandra: We women in the war felt that we made a very important contribution to change, especially considering how women are treated in our present-day society. In the revolution women were claiming better conditions, and that made us stand firm. We can recall the example of many women who were truly very brave, who left us a very noble example of their courage and their principles as women.

Fighting with the FMLN, we hoped to achieve great things, not only for women but for the whole of society in which women play a part. But perhaps the result was not the kind of victory we had hoped for. Everyone sees that we have got something from all that struggle, but the situation is not very secure. We feel that we lack a lot of things as women. We have not managed to attain what we hoped for, because we still feel like we did before the war. We think little has changed. There is a certain insecurity for women.

In the revolution, people forged the value of respect for women. This was very important. Perhaps because of the comradeship, we felt that in the struggle men and women were equal, and that we all had the same capacities. Now, trying to integrate ourselves into normal society, we would like to carry on in the same way, but there are no opportunities. For example, women ex-combatants who can't find a job are going back to the way things were before, to the home, to being a housewife, having children, and that's it. We feel that greater achievements should have been made after all this effort. There are women's organisations — for example here in Perquín and Segundo Montes there is the Women's Communal Movement — and they seek to overcome this, but it is a difficult situation. There are no opportunities which could provide this space for women to struggle. That's why it is necessary to be aware of our situation.

Pamela: Nidia Díaz, one of the FMLN women commanders, has apparently said: 'I don't want to go back to making *tortillas.*' You are telling us that is precisely what is happening — women are going back to making *tortillas*. We have talked to women and to organisations in the capital who are struggling to overcome *machismo*, to establish a new role and respect for women, and I think one thing women can do is join those groups. But, as you say, if there are no opportunities, it is difficult. What are women to do? They need opportunities to work and express themselves in a different way. What can be done?

Sandra: Here in the war zone there is a high proportion of women ex-combatants. But there were no special training opportunities for women. There was general training for combat and for agriculture, and many women received some agricultural training. But many women like me had grown up in the war, we hadn't been used to working the land. Our aims are different: we want to study and, for example, overcome the problem of illiteracy. In the war we didn't have the opportunity to study.

Pamela: So now it would be good to have the chance to study, wouldn't it? Schools, training workshops of some kind?

Sandra: Yes, especially for women. I live in the community of Segundo Montes. Most people of my age and younger have no guidance on how to have a better future. They don't know what being young means. So they get married and have children while they are still very young, and then that is their life, that is what they are left with. If we made a greater effort, things could be different.

A different reality
Marigold: Have you got hope for the future?

Sandra. Yes, I have. It depends on the effort which each person makes for themselves and to encourage others. I've talked to and worked with many young people and we try to guide them. We have to make the effort to move on and not stay as our parents were. We are in another decade where the reality is different. We can overcome this.

There are women's organisations which help with training but I feel that isn't enough. For example, in Segundo Montes there are many women who lost their husbands in the war. They are young widows with children and their future is uncertain because they have no work, no husband to help them, and no way of surviving. There may be a woman with four or five children who didn't live here before the war; if she goes back to her place of origin it means going right back to square one. And if she has no help from any source, it is a sad situation.

I shall keep on working and seeing how I can study and whether I can be of some help in giving training to the young people. I want to collect materials, videos perhaps, that will help in this. I think it is a priority to work in awareness-raising. After so many years of war, when we shared a marginal existence — when we shared victories, sadness and happiness, we helped each other, we saw our comrades die and we were all in it together — now we see everyone going their own way, trying to find a way to make a living.

Pamela: Do you mean there is more individualism now?

Sandra: Yes, although we have started forming cooperatives, some of them with ex-combatants. It is a way of organising projects and production in order to make a living. But now there is more pressure and everyone looks out for themselves, whereas before we were concerned with the welfare of everyone. There haven't been any projects here for the sectors which are most in need, such as the elderly, orphans. The FMLN is going to have a big responsibility, a social burden. But it is a party coming out of war, and it has nothing — and now there are the elections coming up. It is a very complex problem — to understand the situation, to know how to go forward, how to survive.

Andrea
Women's group coordinator, Nueva Esperanza

Andrea and her husband, like many Salvadoreans, went to Honduras in the early 1960s to try to make a living. They prospered there, had a house and a shop, but were thrown out with nothing during the so-called football war between Honduras and El Salvador in 1969. In the 1970s Andrea worked in a team of catechists led by a group of mainly Spanish priests based at the pastoral centre of Los Naranjos in Jiquilisco. Archbishop Romero was then the local bishop and still very conservative. She remembers him saying to the priests: 'When you have awakened the people, what are you going to give them?' 'We are giving them fishing equipment, not fish.' 'And what if it leads to trouble?' 'We hope that you will support us.'

Andrea had weak legs because of childhood polio. She and her husband had no children and adopted a boy who was epileptic and mentally handicapped. Andrea's husband 'disappeared' in 1978; she feels this was because of her activities. Now she lives in the returned refugee community of Nueva Esperanza (New Hope) but, unlike most of its residents, she was not a refugee.

Andrea: I worked during that terrible time of war. The only crime we committed at that time was to be Catholics and to work with base Christian communities, not as a church which just prayed, but as a church where everyone was equal. Our struggle was to liberate the whole person, body and soul, both in their faith and in those things which everyone has a right to. That was the only crime of the catechists in that zone of Jiquilisco where I worked. We had Monseñor Romero here with us in Salinas de Potrero inaugurating a week of mission with the Fathers from Jiquilisco and many friends. We were going round evangelising. But our problem was that our evangelisation was not meant to put people to sleep but to wake them up — that was the motive.

The time when we could evangelise passed. When 1979 came [when the country was moving towards civil war] those of us who were catechists couldn't stay in our homes any more. [The security forces] came to look for us in our houses. So the people who were brave and felt responsible for their people decided to go to the mountains, women and men. Those of us who had some handicap decided to flee to save ourselves. We sheltered here and there in convents or with friends; when they came looking for us, we slipped out another way.

After they killed Monseñor Romero we suffered even greater persecution: they came into convents to search for people because they thought that's where the 'subversives' were. I had taken refuge in this convent myself, as I had been separated from my family two years before. All of them, including the children, had gone to the mountains. They were part of the people known as *masas* who accompanied the guerrillas — entire families went off with them. If they were caught they were killed, whole families. Or else they lost their children as they fled. If the soldiers found the children they sometimes spared them, if they happened to take a fancy to them; otherwise they killed them too. This was the great worry I suffered for the two years that I didn't see my family.

On the run

The priests had given me somewhere to live and some work so that I could earn enough to keep myself. Suddenly – we never knew how they got to know – they [the security forces] came to the convent. I don't know how, but something warned me, something came over me, and I said to the priest: 'Father, I'm going to go early, I'm going to bed.' And he said: 'All right, go then.' As I left the convent a great search began. At that time I had lost my son and I had written a letter of protest to the police, asking them how it could be just that a man who was an invalid, an epileptic who couldn't give service to either side because of his illness, could be mistaken for a guerrilla, pulled off the bus and disappeared, and never seen again by his family or anyone. A man who was grown up but who was still a child, who could fall down in a fit anywhere. In my letter I said that enough was enough, that they should stop their evil-doing. The security forces found this letter and read it. Next to the kitchen I had a basket with some things in it and all my papers, and yet somehow they didn't touch that.

That was how I was spared, but the Fathers of the convent didn't want me to stay with them any longer. 'Andreíta, you simply cannot stay here. It isn't that we don't want to have you, but you will compromise us. They will do something to you and to us.' So I asked them to do me a favour and take me to the bus terminal, because I felt brave enough to go back to my own place. So that's what happened, and I left.

The great repression of 1981
After I had been back home with my sister for two days, the great invasion [of security forces] started. That was in 1981. When they got to my sister's house they asked her: 'What have you done with your daughter? Where have you hidden her?' They were talking about me. She said she hadn't got a daughter, only the little girl who was there and who was her only daughter. 'No', they said, 'your daughter was here and she was seen yesterday.' She denied it but they insisted. They kept her daughter all night up a tree, guarded by dogs so that she couldn't reach her; they were hoping that her sons would come to the house so they could kill them. [The sister had seven sons, all with the guerrillas.] That was early in the night. Later on, one of her sons appeared and they let off a hail of bullets but he managed to escape, wounded in one arm.

About a week later they came again and ambushed another of her sons with some companions in a house. There they killed them and stood guard over them for two weeks until only the dry bones were left, waiting for her or someone else from the family to come and find her son.

The relations, who were looking on from a distance, could see the troops keeping watch, until at last they went away, leaving the bodies dried up. Then the mothers came to collect the remains of their sons and bury them. After that my sister was in despair because her other sons went away, and she followed them. I stayed in her house and managed to stay safe for a while.

One night when I was hiding in the yard of a house, they arrived and took away another woman who was like me, right near where I was. They also took two young men and two blocks away they killed them. They put the woman in the middle and the two young men on either side, and in the morning they were found dead. Seeing this, I asked myself if they had taken her by mistake and it was me they were looking for. I was in a panic, and I escaped through the cordon of soldiers on the highway.

Back in San Salvador a Belgian religious sister said to me: 'If you are brave enough to come and live with me, I'm brave enough to have you.' I said: 'I'm brave enough. It depends on you and how you might feel if one day they do something to me.' 'No, God willing, they won't do anything to you and you'll stay here with me.'

I stayed there another year with her, and nothing happened, everything was quiet. During that year I managed to get in touch with my family again. The priests in Jiquilisco informed me that my family was all right and I shouldn't worry. That was a great relief to me.

The refuges

At that time the various refuges were opening for the thousands of refugees from the *masas* who were arriving. That was when I joined the refugees. Children from my family began to arrive, and I devoted myself to looking after them in the refuge.

Noemí[28] and the Fathers from the convent — who had

28. Sister Noemí of the Little Community, now with the Nueva Esperanza community.

already given me so much support — helped me at that time. In this way I could get into the refuge and care for four sick children whom my family had brought to me because they couldn't move around with them when they were so terribly ill.

We arrived at the refuge in El Despertar. While we were there this girl [her niece Silvia who lives with her as an adopted daughter] was born. She has the name Silvia in memory of Sister Silvia[29] who was killed in 1981. The sisters in charge of that refuge, Noemí, Ana María and many others, were from the Little Community.

When the baby was not even a month old, the army came into the refuge, over the walls, just like that. The night before, there had been a terrific outbreak of shooting all round the house, in which 22 young people were killed. They said it was a confrontation [between the army and the guerrillas] but in the morning it was clear they were all students [not guerrillas]. The driver who drove us when we were ill or when we went to buy food in the market — Juan Antonio — he turned up among the 22 dead. The victims were undressed, in their underclothes; the soldiers had taken them from their houses to kill them there. They found a schoolgirl there in her uniform in the doorway of the church of San Antonio Abad.

We spent that whole day without food inside the refuge. They were harassing the Sisters and asking them for information, and the Sisters didn't want to give it to them. They just said: 'Let's get ready because we've got to get out of this refuge.' We left under the protection of Green Cross ambulances.[30] They evacuated us because we were given a deadline to leave: when an order was given one had to obey, otherwise when the soldiers came back they massacred. There had already been a massacre there in El Despertar, that of Father Octavio[31] and his four companions.

29. Silvia Arriola of the Little Community. See box on page 61.
30. Green Cross: private medical assistance programme, loosely modelled on the Red Cross, which sends teams of young people with basic training to help in accidents or war. Claims to be neutral and apolitical.
31. Father Octavio Ortiz. See page 30.

On the move again

We left with just our clothes, and travelled on foot through the streets of San Antonio Abad in the dark, lit by the headlights of the Green Cross ambulances. The people walked and the children and old people went in the convoys. We had a little food with us. That was how we got to the refuge of San José de la Montaña [at that time the diocesan seminary]. There, because there were so many people, there was not enough water and only a little food, and all of the extra people who arrived suffered a great deal.

Those of us who came from San Antonio were divided among all the refuges in little groups, some here and some there. My children and I were sent to the refuge run by the Sisters of the Assumption in Los Planes de Rendero. We stayed there with them for a long time, but I became ill. I had to look after five children — including the six-month-old baby — as well as do the allotted tasks. I had to get up very early to do the washing and everything else for my children, so that I could then join in the other work, because we all had tasks like cleaning and cooking. I got ill because I couldn't manage it all. So they had to take me out of there and I was shifted from one refuge to another. Things were very hard at that time. The soldiers would come into the refuges to harass people. Life was really fraught.

A crisis of faith

Marigold: Did passing through such terrible experiences affect your faith?

Andrea: I went through a really big crisis. There comes a time when suffering weakens you. I said: 'If there is a God and we believe he is a God of life and is good, why does he allow so many bad things?' Especially when I began to get news that my nephews had been killed, two fallen here, another there, and knowing that the dogs were eating them, and knowing that children were dying of hunger because they couldn't get any food, that sometimes weakens one's faith. But at the same time there were the priests and the sisters, and they really went along hand in hand with many people and said: 'We have got to be people of faith.'

I was on the point of going mad. I was on the point of perhaps doing something terrible to myself. But perhaps the very hope which I used to preach to the people restored me, and I said: 'I musn't collapse.' That gave me courage and I was angry with myself and that helped me.

There were times when the priests had to scold me to make me get my strength back. Sometimes people do foolish things because there is no one to help them — but we did help each other.

That spirit which you see in people who don't belong to you, but who are concerned for you, is what gives strength. And I was on the brink. When I felt alone, I said: 'What is my life worth? Why can't I die instead of so many young people who need to live? Why don't I die and not those young men and women who leave so many children?' Because there have been women in the movement who died leaving four or five children orphaned and whose families have had to bring them up. That was the experience of my sister: four of her sons died and she had to bring up so many orphan grandchildren.

Here in the community is where I have found the greatest support. First, because of the organisation we have here and which, in spite of all the defects, gives us hope that we have a future for these children who are growing up. As for the country, there is still no security, there are still deaths, like the [FMLN] *comandantes* who were killed.[32] There is also the fear that if those go on there is not much hope. Because if the brave men, the young men who are the hope for the future, go on disappearing, what can we do? That's what one wonders. What should we have to do again?

Perhaps there can be reconciliation with some of them, because it was not all of them, was it? They weren't all completely soulless people. But as for forgiveness . . . At the

---

32. Murdered in 1993 when political violence was on the increase.

beginning, when they were signing the peace accords, they talked about 'forgive and forget'. Look, knowing that they took away from you what you most loved . . . through the faith we have as Christians, in my place I can forgive, but forget? Who knows? It's very difficult.

The role of women

Marigold: What has been your experience as a woman? Has your role changed now?

Andrea: I'll tell you about my family, my sisters. You know how much they suffered, one of them especially. When one has come through the time of suffering and into a calmer time, women like her — and even some of us women in this community who have suffered the rough weather — can begin to forget a bit. Not all have had the same experience — each one has her story, the role she played as a woman in the time of war. There are demobilised women and war-wounded women, there are women who were left widows, or alone, with their children, perhaps not because their husband died but because the war itself separated them and they have never managed to get together again.

If we managed to organise ourselves here, as women, we would have a first step towards the future. We would have projects for small farms to raise chickens for food, to have a means of earning and to move forward as women. We were offered funding for a chicken-raising project which was to take the form of a loan with small repayments. This aimed to help women promote themselves, to learn to finance themselves and to work together. We were 20 women ready to form this group, all enthusiastic. Some would sell, some would buy, others look after the chickens. But it's all at a standstill because the present community council won't give us the autonomy to carry out the project ourselves. So we may lose this loan because there are only two women on the council and we haven't got enough support.

Marigold: Are women ready to take on leadership responsibilities on the council?

Andrea: I think they are and we hope that now the council
is being changed there will be more women on it.[33] The
present council wouldn't give us autonomy because they
are afraid that the women will change things.

Marigold: That is a problem for women everywhere.

Andrea: And that's why I say they are a bit afraid of us, that
we'll get out of line. We women who are organised have a
role to play, and we have the right to demand that the
council tell us why they won't let us work with small businesses, to develop ourselves. That's what they were lending
us the money for, and now they say they can't do it because
they have to make these changes. We must hope.

---

33. Shortly after this conversation the community elected a new council of 13
members, of whom six were women.

María Julia Hernández
director of the archdiocesan legal
aid office

Pamela: María Julia, how has the fact of your being a woman affected you in this work?

María Julia: I work in human rights here in the legal aid office. When the archbishop appointed me as director of the office he asked all the clergy and everyone to support me in my work. I have felt supported in my work for human rights. I can't explain it, but I haven't had a problem of not being able to work because of my sex, or of being discriminated against. I have been able to develop. The obstacles have come from another source: the fact that I work for human rights has aroused mistrust about what I am doing, because it is an experiment of enormous power. I have had problems with people refusing to collaborate in the investigation of human rights [abuses], not because I am a woman, but because I am working in the field of human rights. In other words, the conflicts I experience come because of what I am defending, not because of the sex I represent.

That is what I have experienced in the legal aid office of the archbishopric. I have felt the support of those who are sensitive to human rights, those who understand the meaning of respect for the individual. I have felt supported by every social class, every kind of person. The big obstacles are of another kind.

Pamela: Have you observed that the women have great courage in coming forward to make their denunciations?

María Julia: In El Salvador I have found that it has been the lot of the women to go and collect the bones, the bodies of their sons, their husbands, their brothers. Yes, women have denounced [violations] more than men. This is no doubt because most of the victims are men. From the point of view of the victims, the women suffer more in their sex than the men. The women suffer the loss of every value, every right, if the perpetrator is a man. Men denigrate her because she is a woman, they rape her because she is a woman. It is aggression towards the female sex. The examples I have witnessed have made a great impact on me: wombs have been opened and the baby taken out. Or they have been raped, impaled, their brains taken out, they have suffered a series of sexual violations because they are women. These things happen much less in the treatment, however cruel, of men. Men have suffered far less in their sex. Yet it is the first thing that is done to a woman the moment she is captured: she is put in a state of defence-lessness and the first attack is on her sex. It is the women who have suffered most.

As for denunciations, I have seen moving cases of mothers, wives and daughters showing great courage to make denunciations and follow them up. There are mothers who have not resigned themselves to the disappearance of their sons and who are still asking: 'Where are they?' I have seen the courage of women seeking information about their children.

Pamela: It must have been very valuable for them to have a woman like you here in the legal aid office.

María Julia: The pastoral work in human rights that I have carried out in the church — being with the victims, helping them, listening to their case, following it up and investigating it — I think it has been a support for the people who come to this office. They haven't felt that they are in a vacuum, where nobody can explain things to them or help them. People know that there is a space for them here.

Sisters Patricia Farrell and Peggy O'Neill
North Americans working in
Suchitoto

The town of Suchitoto in the department of Cuscatlán, close to the Guazapa volcano, was one of the first to suffer persecution. This was because of the pastoral activity of its priests and their training of lay leaders, in line with the new model of church proclaimed at Medellín in 1968. It was at an open air Mass in Suchitoto that Archbishop Romero first spoke with prophetic force in defence of the peasants' right to organise.

Patricia Farrell: It's a hard time here right now, a very hard time. It's the exhaustion, post-war trauma. It's having to realise that the gains were minimal materially, having to realise that the rebuilding is another kind of struggle. There is also a psychological let-down at every level, which is a key part of the process. Yet to a certain degree people haven't been allowed to just let down.

Women's groups in the FMLN
We started here in Guazapa, in one of the zones where the FMLN began to organise. It's been a unique place in the country, because as the war was beginning and the organising was starting, all five groups of the FMLN were represented in Guazapa.[34] For the most part the different groups grew up separately, in different geographical pockets, and then came together in an umbrella organisation, the FMLN, but all five groups were represented here.

This zone was particularly hard hit during the

---

34. The five groups of the FMLN were: Ejército Revolucionario del Pueblo (ERP — People's Revolutionary Army); Fuerzas Populares de Liberación (FPL — Popular Liberation Forces); Resistencia Nacional (RN — National Resistance); Partido Revolucionario de los Trabajadores Centroamericanos (PRTC — Central American Workers' Revolutionary Party); and Fuerzas Armadas de Liberación (FAL — Armed Liberation Forces). ERP and RN have now separated from the FMLN.

repression, and for all practical purposes it emptied, except for the town of Suchitoto, where there were at one point only 50 families that stayed out of 15,000 people. Of the 32 towns and villages of the zone, 30 were completely destroyed, and all the people left. When we came back here in March 1988, six communities had been repatriated; now there are 60. People come back in droves, so we've been doing general pastoral work as refugees return, and one community after another builds up again.

It's been interesting to see the women's movement mushroom here in El Salvador. Peggy O'Neill and I have been interested in women's issues all along — we are probably the only religious in the country who have closely accompanied the whole women's movement. We have tried to reflect the particular reality of the zone, because there are lots of divisions, particularly on the left. Some of them have to do with money, funding, competition, with one group getting more than another. We've watched the women of the left go through different struggles about how closely to identify with their parent political group of the FMLN. Some have concluded they want to be autonomous.

At the moment, four out of the five groups of the FMLN are represented in the zone where we work, and every one of them has a corresponding women's group. The divisions among those groups have deep historical roots — they are coming out of a long process that we have not lived through with them.

We have tried to be supportive of the liberation process of the people, without identifying with any one group, and that has sometimes been a disadvantage. We have a little less credibility with all the groups than we would if we were identified with any one of them. They trust more completely the people who give them their total allegiance, which we have not done. In other ways it's been an advantage, because it gives us a broader convoking power in the zone. When only one group calls a meeting, they tend only to get people from that political group, but when we in the parish call a meeting, we get attendance from across all the political lines. So we've tried hard to maintain that. We have helped the women form a coalition of women's organisations to go beyond the divisions. I find the women so much more open to that than the men. I really think unity is going to come much faster and more naturally and spontaneously to the women — not that it's not difficult, the roots of historical divisions run deep.

Developing unity
We formed the Women's Movement of Cuscatlán in this zone. Seeing that funding was often a root cause of division, we tried to look for common funding for projects. We are in the middle of launching a literacy project for women representing all the political groups in the zone — we have materials from Nicaragua that use generative words[35] that are about consciousness-raising on women's issues. We have done some mental health work with women and some work with sex education and basic formation [education and training], always with the aim of bringing together the women of different political lines. To me, one of the most satisfying things has been to see friendships develop among women of different groups. When they are friends, it is harder to break down their allegiance than when it is based on some abstract notion that we should all work together.

Language and symbol
We have tried in small ways to make an issue of sexist language, but we found it artificial, so we haven't pushed it too hard. What we have done is try to create situations where the language is symbol and gesture, which is more universal, more feminine, and communicates at a deeper level than words. This culture is very verbal, very wordy. These poor people are subjected to long political discourses: a *comandante* will get up and talk at them ad infinitum, and they accept that, because they know no other

---

35. 'Generative' is a term used by Paulo Freire for the significant words which he used as a basis for literacy classes, and also as themes for discussion.

way. It's the same in church — they expect to have 45-minute sermons, which we find very oppressive, but they accept it as normal. Too many words.

So, both pastorally and in our work with women, we try to use ritual and symbol and gesture. It was clear to us at the time of the signing of the peace accords that there were mixed feelings among the people. Almost everyone we talked to said they came to the celebration of the peace accords with a lump in their throats, because it instantly brought to mind the people who were not there to celebrate that moment with them, the people who had died along the way. Somehow that particular juncture became the point at which people, maybe for the first time, began really to remember the dead, and in some way began to mourn them. We found it important to create spaces for mourning, through gestures and so on. In the celebrations of the word that we helped design for Lent and Holy Week, we deliberately structured in moments when they could name their dead and talk about them.

We found the use of gesture and ritual and symbol a natural form of expression for the women — they can't get interested in sexist language, but when you offer them an alternative to so many words, they respond.

An outpouring of grief

One of the first things we did in Copapayo — where they repatriated from Mesa Grande in Honduras — was to celebrate Mother's Day. We had a big pan, the kind that they cook *tamales* [dumplings] in, full of water, everyone had a big red flower, and we put out a statue of a woman breastfeeding a child, and had three readings to help us talk about God as a source of nourishment. The symbol of a mother breastfeeding her child is a very good Eucharistic symbol of God who wants to nourish us. So we talked about that very briefly and then asked the women to put their flower in the water and say their mother's name. (At another point there was a gesture to remember their children.) The first person put her flower in the water and said her mother's name and the whole group started to cry. There was half an hour of crying.

It was one of the first experiences which made us realise how necessary it is to give people space and permission to allow some of their feeling about what has happened in the years of war to surface. The lid has been put on so much. Part of the attitude during the war, at least on the left, was that if you mourned too much, it was a sign that you were not 'aware', not 'committed'. The women have responded particularly sensitively to the opportunities for expressing grief.

The need for spiritual depth
Last year was the first time in Suchitoto that we celebrated International Women's Day. Part of our effort here has been to give special emphasis to the peasant women, because the women's movement in El Salvador is pretty much dominated by urban women. The leadership is with women in the capital, and our reality here is all peasant women. Most Salvadorean women are peasants. When you go to any of the meetings, the leadership tend to speak — urban women are more educated, more vocal. So we try to give confidence to these women who have never had a voice, and encourage them to do a lot locally. In a lot of small ways we have tried to give them opportunities to speak, about anything at all.

I don't think the women's movement will go anywhere unless it is inserted into a larger cosmic canvas and rooted in some kind of spiritual depth. A new definition of spirituality is needed, otherwise it won't have the momentum to carry through into the future. Overcoming patriarchy is not enough.

This is a very discouraging historical moment [after the peace accords], there's no vision today, there's an emptiness. But this is not going to last, it's a time of gestation. We have to trust the fallow field, that something fertile is gestating there. It's very important to keep hope alive.

The age of the Spirit
Pamela: What do you think is the role of Mary in all this?

Patricia: Mary's role needs to be redefined. And I also think we need to move away from Jesus a little more. There is a real poverty of theology of the Spirit. We are in the age of the Spirit and the church needs to shift its focus off Jesus and place it more on the Spirit, which can be given a more feminine interpretation.

Jesus Christ was incarnated in a masculine body, there is no way of refuting that historically — but this is not the age of Jesus, this is the age of the Spirit. I think it's another expression of patriarchy that there is such a poverty of theology of the Spirit in the church.

The theology of the real
Peggy O'Neill: I'm here in Suchitoto for only six months every year. I go home to the United States for six months, and try to stimulate theological reflection with young students at a liberal arts college, Iona, in New York. My reflecting has always come from who I am, from my experience of life, even before I left the United States and came to El Salvador. I think that's why I got my doctorate in religious education rather than theology: I didn't want to be caught in a system of thinking, I wanted to think theologically from where I was standing or with whom I was standing. I felt the need to be broader-based in reflection, so that it was not up in the sky.

Coming to a place like El Salvador for the past couple of years and living with people here has intensified my awareness that this is the only way to do this kind of reflection. I've come to appreciate the fact that liberation theology is a method and it is the method that really is the key to the future. That is why I think other people criticise it so much. They don't perceive it as a real theology because it seems only to speak about the real, not in abstractions. I think the problem is that we can't control the results of the reflection if we hand ourselves over to the Spirit. God is always acting in the human situation, we collide with God in the real world, it is the only place. I don't consciously talk about El Salvador in the United States — but my students know I'm speaking out of an experience that has altered my vision and my behaviour and this gives them the freedom to take their own experiences seriously. They find that liberating. Somehow I become for them a symbol that it's possible to say: 'I have something to reflect on.' This is important when you're only 21 or 22 and you think there is no way you can do God-talk, because you don't know the terminology.

Here in El Salvador you don't have to give people permission to talk about God in their lives, because they haven't been locked into another way of thinking. They have no habit of thinking that the academic naming of God is the only way you name God, whereas my students, coming out of academic institutions, somehow sense that. Here you don't have to take the first step, you can just jump in because people are always standing in the midst of life — life surrounds them so. There aren't any distractions from the real here.

There was a time when the church controlled the interpretation of scripture; then all of a sudden the academy,[36] using the scientific tools of language studies, excavations and so on, began to come up with new interpretations. The academy was the only interpreter for a while, and it wanted to loosen what was a controlled interpretation by the church. But once you put these books into the hands of people who interpret them in their own way, you find that the academy itself is committing the sin it tried to correct [ie controlling the interpretation].

Never drop anchor

Once you have a set of canons, it means constant interpretation. You can never drop anchor. You are on a ship and

---

36. Academy. This does not refer to any specific institute but to the academic study of biblical texts which aimed to offer an interpretation different from that provided by the church.

you can't say — as the church and then the academy said — 'Drop your anchor here, you can't go to another port. That's it. We've found it.' Now, I don't want to bypass all that wonderful research of the early church, and the church in the Middle Ages; all those kinds of interpretations are wonderful. The boat can go back and forth, but it can't drop anchor. The tools are the same but clearly it's going to be a different verbalisation in El Salvador now from what it was in the 1980s. They have to know that that's OK, this needs to be on-going. It's never not going to be liberation — that is what it is all about, it will always be that. It means developing a spirituality that will sustain us, no matter where the ship is sailing or what port we seem to be hovering in.

Pamela: But there's going to be a different kind of dialogue between the person and the word of God as we move along. Revelation is in a sense going to change.

The dance of the Spirit
Peggy: We can catch ourselves in the changes now. We had a delegation here the other day, and a woman wondered whether we need to name a different theology. Again, I think we keep forgetting that liberation theology is a method, it doesn't really need a new name. It can have a new name but we aren't looking for one. The point is that we must face the real, and not silence the voice of God or the manifestation of the holy in the midst of reality, or to put it another way, not terminate the dance of the Spirit. The Spirit is in this eternal dance, and we must somehow move wherever the partner in the dance is moving.

The women of Suchitoto

We arranged to meet some of the women with whom Pat Farrell and Peggy O'Neill worked, and drove out to Suchitoto again a few days later. Prominently displayed on the wall of the meeting room was an honorary degree from Iona College in New York. This had been presented to two of the women, Mercedes and Carmen, in May 1993 on behalf of all the women in this zone of Guazapa.

It reads as follows (translation):

> After 12 years of civil war and 80,000 dead, with 1 million Salvadoreans in exile and 800,000 displaced inside the country, Salvadoreans continue to believe that life and not death will have the last word. For Salvadorean men, resistance meant the will to die rather than surrender. For Salvadorean women, resistance meant refusing to let the community die. The central drama of the lives of these women is not about how to die, but how to live. They continue giving witness to the insurrection of life in the face of death, of compassion in the midst of hatred, of truth in the face of lies. The daily search of women in the Guazapa zone is for enough corn to make *tortillas* and for a new voice in history. A dialectic of persecution and ingenuity born out of necessity has marked these women with a consciousness that transforms individualism. The story of their lives reveals the creative power of a shared life, its ability to heal the broken heart and smashed body of a people. By definition these women are poor, having neither house nor land; they are nevertheless the animators of the communities,

architects of social cohesion, agents of a new humanity. They are the political organisers, pastoral agents, martyrs and activists [militants] who struggle to create a new history, a new woman, a new church. For their ability to carry the suffering of an entire people, for their just indignation before so much injustice and poverty, for their courageous contribution to the fight for liberation and peace in El Salvador, Iona College confers on the Women of Guazapa the degree of Doctor of Humanities, Honoris Causa.

Mercedes and Carmen went to New York to accept the degree in the name of all the women of the Guazapa zone.

On their return to El Salvador there was a celebration at which more than 100 women took turns at dressing up in a cap and gown and having their photograph taken. A copy of the honorary degree has been framed and hung in every community in the zone. Patricia Farrell comments. 'We have hundreds of "doctors" here!'

Carmen was one of the women we met in Suchitoto. Originally from the department of Cabañas, she is now in the community of Copapayo and is president of the women's organisation in her community. Carmen has three daughters and one son; three other sons who joined the guerrillas were killed in combat. When Carmen told us her story, all the women wept.

Mercedes was the first woman in the zone to become the president of the executive of her whole community.

The conferring of the degree represented a recognition of the worth of those on the underside of history. The stories of kings and queens, the presidents and generals, the 'important' people whose exploits used to fill the history books, are giving way to the stories of peasants, the refugees, the shanty-town dwellers, the farmers, the ordinary soldiers, sailors and candle-stick makers whose lives are the basis of history.

The women had all shared the experiences and heard each

other's stories, probably many times over. But the need to remember, not to allow the past to be buried, kept them intently listening to each speaker, occasionally murmuring assent, supplying a place name or a date, reliving the events described. Since the dominant power, including the ecclesial power, often tries to get people to forget the past, to be 'reconciled', this remembering, this refusal to let the official version be the sole version, is truly subversive.

The presence of God

Lucía O (a member of the pastoral team): We have a lot of experience of the presence of God in ourselves, in the war and afterwards. God has worked many miracles for me — the women here know that.

The biggest miracle God performed for me was during a *guinda*, a flight from our canton to another department. We had a *guinda* from here in Cuscatlán to the department of Santa Ana, with thousands of people walking for a day and night. We were walking under fire, because there were 12,000 soldiers in those operations in Guazapa. Their mission was to eliminate the people in that area, to massacre us. The operation was known as Guazapa 10. We suffered so much in that operation that only those of us who went through it can believe it. But, the *muchachos* were smart. They used to tell us: 'You have to keep going, keep going, keep going, so that when the army comes they won't find anyone here.'

We were in the mountains, with crowds of people, when they told us: 'You must leave immediately, they are coming to kill.' The people ran as fast as they could, with children and bundles. We went by the water's edge, not along the flat land, but in the ravines, through bombs and gunfire. The soldiers were already there on the hills, and we were surrounded. We kept going until we reached a dark ravine, and we waited for night to come to get out. Our guides felt helpless. What were they going to do with all these people? But we had hope to go on living.

One of my sons, Peter, was one of the leaders. He called

us and said: 'We are going to leave this zone, there's no other way, and we're going along a road that we don't know, to a place we don't know.' They gave us a whole lot of instructions — not to make a noise, to get strength to walk.

So we left, and we walked and walked, we passed the paved road, the open sewer, and the cane fields of Cabañas. At one point we had to lie down and they told us: 'Don't get up, even if you hear shots, don't get up.' I thought we were going to die, it was the end. But the soldiers didn't come. The *muchachos* were here, you see [indicating different positions], we were there, and the armed forces came that way. They began firing — their aim was not to kill the guerrillas, but to kill the people. So we were close by, but we didn't die. I think that was a miracle.

We had a celebration to give testimony to the faith, because we are witnesses of the faith and of the miracles of Christ.

'It's hard to know God'

During the offensive they told me my son was dead. This was the terrible offensive in San Salvador, when all the young men were taken to fight. They had taken my son, and from the moment he went, I said: 'Will he come back, or won't he?' I kept asking God to look after him, that if he fell wounded there would be someone to help him. I appealed to the heart of Jesus, and 12 days passed without hearing anything about him.

Then some of the men came back, and I asked them: 'Have you seen Osmaro?' 'No, we saw him in the beginning, but not after.' Then they told my husband: 'Osmaro has fallen.' His knapsack and his rifle were there, because he had fallen. He was dead. That night how I cried! I felt I had gone mad — but always with faith. I prayed: 'If he has fallen wounded, let someone pick him up and take him to the hospital.'

And that's what happened. He was wounded, he walked and found some poor families on the outskirts of

San Salvador, and they helped him. He was stumbling, wounded. Some of you have seen the wound in his head. He has a hole in his head where he lost a lot of blood. He says that a woman and a man picked him up, they gave him a cup of coffee and took him to a clinic and then to the Rosales hospital. And I didn't know! We were beginning the prayers [traditionally recited for nine days after a death] because we thought he was dead. But I had faith, I didn't want to take part in the prayers. I kept on saying: 'He isn't dead, he isn't dead.'

After 12 days, thank God, a lady from Palacios went to the hospital looking for her uncle who had also been wounded. She recognised my son and he knew her. He got up and he said: 'Look, señora, tell my mother to bring me my papers and my clothes', because his clothes were all covered in blood. So this lady sends a friend to tell me that Osmaro is in the hospital and wants clothes.

I felt my heart beating and I went off and asked the lady who had sent the message if it was true. 'Yes, he's in hospital. He can't leave because he has no clothes or documents.' If he went out without documents he would be arrested. So I went to the hospital with the lady. When I saw him I made an effort not to cry, because there were police there watching him. So I bent over him, I didn't even speak, I hadn't the strength to speak. He was very pale.

So it all came out well. It's God. I say to some people that it's hard to know God like that, and there we knew God. We knew him there even more than before. I say we are witnesses of faith. We have something to confirm and increase people's faith.

I say that we can see him — he shows himself in a little bird or in a tree. I tell people that we saw God in the war and after the war. The sisters came to us during the war — who would have believed that people would come to us from so far away? God was coming in these women. We were frightened when they came, and some said: 'These are the people who caused the war' [because they came from the United States]. Then they introduced themselves and asked me if we wanted to work. 'Of course,' I said, rather frightened. There was no doctrine being taught then and the children were growing up without anything, so I told people: 'These women are a gift of God.'

Monseñor Romero saved me

Bernarda belongs to the executive of the Women's Movement of Cuscatlán. On 22 August 1982, 200 people — men, women and children — were massacred in El Calabozo on the river Amatitán, department of San Vicente.[37] Bernarda survived the slaughter.

Bernarda: You mentioned Amatitán. I survived that massacre. My little girl and I survived. My husband left me because he said they were going to kill him — they were killing everyone then. They lined up the children, then the women and the old people. I buried myself in the ground and threw grass over my little girl and me. I was giving her my breast and had taken it away, but then I gave it to her again.

I kept saying: 'The blessed blood of Monseñor Romero. The blessed blood of Monseñor Romero' — but to myself, not out loud. While the soldiers went to get petrol to throw over the 300 bodies of children, women and old men that were lying there, I escaped to a place a little further off. I went seven days without eating, but what you can't endure is not having water. I feel that Monseñor Romero saved me from that massacre.

Later, I had a little boy who was deaf and dumb. I took him to the best specialists and my little boy didn't get better, they said his ear drums had broken and the infection had spread. I became discouraged and I went to cry at the tomb of Monseñor Romero, and I told him about my son, I gave him his name. Now my son can talk and hear. He's called Oscar Arnulfo, Monseñor Romero's name. He hears, he speaks, he goes to second grade, he is big and dark.

---

37. Truth Commission 1993, *op cit.*

I think our testimony must also remember the four North American religious.[38] We shouldn't forget them because they were brave women and they died with us. I always say: 'Monseñor Romero, the four religious and the others, nearly 100,000.'[39] So that is my little testimony. If we were strong in those days, we can be stronger today.

God lifted us up

Lucía B (works with the Committee in Defence of Women): I can't say much about the Bible because I am not very well educated. But as to faith in God, from all that we have suffered, there have been moments . . . We haven't seen him as a person in front of our eyes, but we have seen his miracles, and sometimes we have heard him spiritually in our bodies. As if God lifted us up by his power and put us somewhere else.

I was at the massacre of Zacamil in 1982. It was a terrible massacre — I saw the death squads from about half a block away, they were going to take me to shoot me to pieces. I managed to get us away. I got my mother-in-law away — she was an old lady. We managed to escape. During the other terrible massacre, here in Guadalupe, the bombs fell on us, near us, lifting us up. We were deafened by the bombardment and the shelling. After that we were hungry and thirsty day and night, we hadn't houses or anything. I gave birth to a daughter at five o'clock in the morning and at seven I was fleeing through the grass because they were chasing us. I was running without food. They gave me roots to eat. After five days we ran into Operation Phoenix.[40]

Then they captured me, with four children. They

---

38. The four North American church women were Ita Ford, Maura Clarke, Dorothy Kazel and Jean Donovan, murdered in El Salvador on 2 December 1980.
39. The figure usually given for the number of people who died in El Salvador's civil war is 75,000, the majority of them civilians killed by the armed forces.
40. Operation Phoenix (January-March 1986) was conducted by the Salvadorean armed forces on the Guazapa volcano, resulting in the deaths of 245 people, mostly women, elderly people and children. Some 1,045 civilians were taken to the Calle Real displaced persons camp near the capital; 445 houses, 100 acres of cornfield, 17 acres of banana trees and harvested sorghum and maize were destroyed.

wanted to kill me. But a sergeant said: 'No, don't kill this woman. Take her to the camp where the other people are. There', he said to me, 'you will see all the people we have.' I answered that it was lies, that it wasn't so. But, when I got there, I saw all the people, many of them known to me.

From there they put me in a helicopter and took me to Sanchico. They kept me there for about a week. I had no family to come and claim me, as my husband had stayed here in the hills. The soldiers took my photo and my family saw it in the paper, but they couldn't come and claim me because they were afraid. They hoped the soldiers would kill me there, so that I wouldn't return.

But the soldiers didn't want to let me go, because I had another little girl of about nine months, and one of them wanted to take her away from me. I didn't want to give her to him and the stupid man said that unless I gave her to him, they wouldn't let me go. So I told them they could do what they liked with me, they could kill me or anything, but I wasn't going to give them my little girl.

Then at about 11 at night a sergeant came with a type-writer, and said: 'Look, tomorrow we can let you go, but you will sign here and give him the little girl. He will be her father, and take her away, and you can go.' I said: 'You can keep me here. I can die here, but I won't give you the little girl and I won't sign. The little girl is mine and I am not giving her away.' Then the soldier said: 'You are still breastfeeding her. If you give her to me, I will take her to my father's farm, in Santa Ana. You can work there and we will pay you the month's work and when you have weaned the baby, if you want to go you can go, and leave the child with me.' I said: 'No way.'[41]

The Lord helped me. A friend from here, from Plantanares, came and recognised me and said: 'I am going to take you away and get you out. I'll come back.' She came back in the afternoon.

---

41. The Asociación Pro-Búsqueda de los Niños (Association in Search of Children) has documented 213 cases of 'disappeared' children since 1993 and found a total of 24.

Women are important in our society

Pamela: Bernarda, how do you see the role of women now in El Salvador?

Bernarda: The other day I was in the community of Papaturro. I was telling them that women are important in our society, that we are part of development, integral to it, body and soul, and that men and women together are going to push forward the development of the communities. I told them that without God there could be no real development of the communities. I noticed that there was quite a lot of understanding in the community when I was talking about this. Some of us were crying — Juanita here could tell you.

We relate the Gospel to the real life we are living, not to those far-off times. We see how we live in the grass shack, the corrugated iron hut, we see the barefoot, malnourished children, and we see the mother who has perhaps been able to get some little thing from the hills that she can cook for them. She has only had one *colón* in the whole day. So we see that we women are good, capable managers in the home, because if we have five *colones* we get vegetables, food, a small pastry.

We also try to get the women to believe in themselves, that they are strong, good fighters, that they have power to change. Society has put it into our unconscious that we aren't capable, that in order to earn a position we must sacrifice ourselves. For example, in the war we had to do tasks that the men were frightened to do, but we had the courage to do them, we had the courage to die. Today, some are passive, but we here in Suchitoto are not passive. We are seeing Christ with the eye as the saying goes, where things are going well, where we fit in. They have always put us in the private spaces, so we are opening the public spaces too. We have two women up as candidates for mayor here in Cuscatlán, so now we have to support these women. We must organise and train a brigade of women so that when they come to govern, they govern for the women. When they see that we women support them now, they should be conscious of gender issues later.

Pamela: The question of the private or public role of women is interesting. How do you see the role of Mary in the church?

Bernarda: They say Mary was a seamstress, so they put her in the traditional work of the home. But she also went to the synagogue, she went to the wedding of Cana and got her son to change the water into wine, she spoke up in defence of her son: she had a public role. Yet when we here spoke up in defence of our sons they accused us of being political. And Mary Magdalen was the first to say that Jesus was not in the tomb — we women are smarter than the men — that's what she told them, and the men didn't believe. The men didn't go, they were passive.

Carmen: I am glad to have this meeting with these sisters, so that we can tell them the important place that the women have had in this country, in this process. Here in El Salvador there hasn't been an appreciation of the role of women, and now we are trying to get this into people's heads. We are still submissive, we haven't got out of it, and we want to get out.

Confronting *machismo*
Julia (represents the women of Copapayo): We women in the countryside have lived a situation of oppression, beginning in the home. The man wants to keep you under control – 'If I want you to, you can go out; if not, not.' This happened to me. I have had big problems in my house with my husband, fighting him whole nights without sleeping, because I am in this process, fighting the situation. He was against it. I had a daughter of 15 and I made her realise the situation we have in this country, so the two of us used to attack him. 'Dad,' we said, 'people in this country — beginning with you — don't think we are worth anything.'

But we are worth something, we have the same understanding, the same values you have.'

We opened the Bible and there we saw the injustice women live under in this country — as men live under oppression, the women do too. In *Hosea*, look what Hosea says! And not only to the men, he means it in general terms. So our decision is that we live together, or separate. That's the task. For life, or for death, we're going to do it. We're not afraid of death, because if we have to die for justice we'll die. I said I would die for this — and here I am. My daughter died at 17, they killed her. And she was so good for our work in this process. But you know what we have lived through, it's been so hard.

Julia gives a talk

Here in the Department of Cabañas, in Cinquera, there was a big meeting, where I gave a talk. I worked for two nights to prepare this talk, and I presented it to the priest, Father Miguel Flores. 'Father,' I said, 'I've prepared this talk. I don't know whether you agree with it'. He read it and said: 'Magnificent, Julia. Do it.'

In my talk I told everyone about the importance of women in El Salvador, that this is not recognised, and that in this country we are used as instruments of pleasure and business. If you go to San Salvador and look at the big shops, there is the woman with her naked body, her big legs, presenting Morazán cigars. If we go to a place selling car tyres, there's the woman with her legs crossed, naked, to give value to the tyres. It's terrible. I don't think our bodies should be used to give value to tyres, to cigars. That's what we've been used for in this country, only business. But to get people to see our situation at home — nothing.

What else are we used for? As servants. Stuck in those big houses in San Salvador, young, pretty, well turned out, because we have been alienated. What that one does, I can do. If you are wearing a pretty dress, I'll wear one too. That sort of alienation — we have been very simple. Then the

> Women are also the ones who suffer the most in the coffee plantations, because they are the ones who pick coffee. They work as a family group and receive a miserably low wage. They go to the coffee plantation with their five children, the women pick the coffee and their children collect it and clean it — in other words the whole family works. But the owner of the coffee plantation doesn't acknowledge this. He only pays the woman for what she picks, and gives her a *tortilla* with beans to give to the five children.
>
> From Isabel Ramírez, 'Opening a Door to Women in El Salvador',
> in *Challenge*, Vol 1, No 3, Spring 1992.

master falls in love with the servant: 'Come here to the bedroom.' Suddenly, the big tummy. When she returns to the house she is seen differently. The mistress didn't realise the situation. But on seeing the difference in the maid: 'Go home because I don't like your taking my husband.' These are big problems.

Who suffers in these situations? Our mothers, because we take them the burden of children. We haven't earned, we have suffered — we go home with the children.

Another job to earn money is the coffee harvest. You should have seen how we used to sleep on the estates. On the floor, among the rubbish — then carrying the sacks of coffee on your back, sometimes it rains and the coffee gets all muddy, your heads gets all greasy and muddy, and your hands all roughened. The foreman used to say to us: 'You people are horrible!' At midday we would be given two little *tortillas*, with a few beans and a cockroach on top.

Arrested

I told the people the whole story of what we went through, and they cried, they were moved, it was the reality of what we were living in the country. But while I was saying all this, the police arrived and took me off. 'This woman is a subversive, she's come to get the women to lift their heads. But they are quite happy.' I had been on the run for a long time, because the men of my canton were pursuing me. Every night they watched my house, every day they watched to see where I was going, where I was coming from, what I was doing. They watched me until I went to bed. Then they arrested me and the National Police of San Salvador held me for five days with my eyes bandaged with bits of dirty pants, so that I couldn't see to right or left. I was handcuffed with two other women. It was a place where they massacred men, there were a lot of men and women there — I couldn't see but I heard talking. It was a place of torture and the men shouted, cried out. They took me to a room where they took all my clothes off, in front of a man, with the police outside on guard, and he searched me as if I had been his woman. I felt terrible in my heart. He asked me: 'Why did you get organised?' 'Because I've read the Bible and Jesus says that we must not be silent, because the sin we are living is serious.'

Reading the Bible leads to trouble

When I read the Bible, people who opposed us lifted their legs and farted. Yes, the men farted, spat, shouted, stoned us — that was what we went through when we read the Bible.

The man who was getting information from me asked what book I had read. I said: 'The 58th chapter of *Isaiah*, where he says, "Woe to those men who go about molesting people! Woe to those who pile up house on house, field on field, without seeing the situation other people live in."' And chapter 25 of *Matthew* when Jesus comes to judge everyone. So that Christ should not condemn us, we used to read the chapter to see if we could change the situation. We used to read the Bible, we used to sit under mango trees, because men were going round spying, you see, to catch us out. The one who was questioning me asked why I read those chapters. 'Well, it's the Bible and I have to read it.' From the first chapter of *Genesis* up to the Apocalypse, we've read it.

Pamela: I would like to hear from others about reading the Bible, because I think it is a key point. The Bible can lead to problems, can't it, as you have seen in your lives.

Enoe works with the women's secretariat in Progreso and is a member of the Christian Committee for the Displaced in El Salvador (CRIPDES).

Enoe: My faith began when I was very small. My father was a good Catholic, but he died when he was about 25. I was about three. With my father dead my mother had no aim in her life; she sold everything my father had left, and she went wandering off with us three children. But when I was about 12 I began to give catechism classes in the canton where we lived. I liked religion and I liked singing from the book that the sisters here know well. Later, people began to organise in the cantons because where we lived there was a lot of poverty. There were big landowners with a lot of land, and in exchange for work they gave people somewhere to live. I also belonged to the Legion of Mary with a group of young people, nearly all of them girls. Some seminarians came to see us; all the people of the canton met in the main church and read texts from the Bible. Then the seminarians distributed bits of the Bible, from the readings, and we discussed them in groups. We commented on them at length, based on real life, on the life we were living then, the poverty, oppression. So it was that we began discussing the Bible and this motivated me. I had always, since I was small, asked why there were rich and poor, why some of us lived so wretchedly — sometimes at school I had to pick up the bits of pencil other children had thrown away so that I could go on writing. I asked myself why this was, and I wanted to find a way of changing it.

The Bible wakes you up
Then those seminarians said this could be changed, that the poor had not been born poor; we were poor because of the system we lived under. I woke up, and said: 'Yes, there is a

way of changing this.' We had always been told that the poor were poor and there was nothing we could do to change it. We would get our reward in the next life. We would find the kingdom of God in the next world, and the rich wouldn't because they would pay there for what they had done to us. But when the seminarians said it wasn't like that, but that we had to struggle to change the situation, I felt wonderful, that we could go ahead and do something.

At that time the security forces began to persecute people who read the Bible and those of us who were cate-chising. They persecuted us. The great persecution began against religious people. I remember they told our group: 'They will shut you up in the church with that Bible!'

Then with a group – Carmen was one of them – we began to work as women. I like it very much, although it is quite difficult. It is difficult for us women to organise, above all to be able to take women out of the house — from all the tasks we have to carry out in the home, looking after the children, doing everything in the house. There is no help. It is difficult, it costs, it is a complicated task. But we were strong during the war, they threatened us, they bombed us and shelled us, and we went ahead and did a lot to change the situation. So we can go on in the same way now. It is a struggle that has gone on for centuries, but if we don't begin to claim our rights and ask that we be respected as human beings too, nothing will happen. One way or another we have to face up to this situation. Together.

As we left the meeting, Peggy pointed out a woman sitting on the sidewalk a few yards away; she got up and moved off as we looked at her. Peggy explained that the woman had 'put the finger' on several people — betrayed them to the security forces — who were later murdered, but the other women bore her no malice. 'They have forgiven her. They know she did it for money because she was poor.'

By contrast, during the meeting, an ARENA electioneering van had passed by in the street, loudspeaker blaring, whereupon several women rushed out into the street shouting: 'Murderers! You killed my family!' They are able to forgive individuals whose situation they understand, but not the structures of violence and oppression.

From a letter from Pat Farrell to Pamela Hussey, July 1994:
Very busy here. Today we inaugurated a three-day-a-week centre for battered women. Little by little things progress. It's a low morale time here after elections, an important moment pastorally, to give hope.

The story of Doña Isabel
Guarjila, Chalatenango

Guarjila is a repopulated community of more than 2,000 people who returned to Chalatenango from the refugee camp in Mesa Grande, Honduras. A Jesuit priest, Jon Cortina, who is chaplain to the communities there, introduced us to two women, both remarkable in their different ways: Doña Isabel and Suyapa.

While we spoke to Doña Isabel on the verandah of her house, her young grandson clambered all over her. Her two daughters were busy about household chores, washing clothes and kitchen utensils, and making *tortillas*.

Pamela: Doña Isabel, will you tell us a little of your personal history, about when you left El Salvador for Honduras, and when you returned?

Doña Isabel: We had to leave our town, Arcatao, on the border with Honduras, in 1981. When I lived there I had no work in the church, because at that time scarcely any women participated. There was a Mass every Saturday and Sunday, but the priest only talked about sin. He never said the people were important, or any of the things we needed to hear.

Then we left for the frontier. I spent two years in Valladolid, and I joined the other women working for the church. There the church was organised. Some Sisters of the Oblates [of the Sacred Heart] used to come and we worked with them.

Then we went to Mesa Grande where there were seven refugee camps and we worked there. We organised ourselves in different sectors: I was responsible for coordinating the different tasks and I had a key to the store of materials for the group. They trusted me and gave me the key so that I could give out what was needed. That's how we worked. I always had a lot of responsibility. I was one of the first to come back [to El Salvador] in 1987. We've gone on organising here; we have a pastoral worker responsible for each sector. This one has 40 families and there is always someone in charge. Each sector has catechists and a pastoral leader who leads reflections once a week. The catechists and others are responsible for keeping an eye on the families in each sector, because people could be left out of the group.

On Sunday 72 young people were confirmed. Bishop Alas came from Chalatenango. He doesn't like coming here. We've invited him several times but he doesn't like coming.

Pamela: Why? Doesn't he feel at home with the people?

Doña Isabel: I think he feels he is different from us. He doesn't think much of our ideals. He comes from one of those families who don't share our principles.

Pamela: Not like Monseñor Romero. Did you know him?

Doña Isabel: Yes. Monseñor Romero was a very dedicated man. He often came here. We knew him. He was what he ought to be, what the church ought to be. The people know his story, he used to go among the poor. But today there isn't one like him.

The last time he went to Arcatao was 24 August 1978 — I remember it well. When he arrived the police searched him, even his shoes, they turned his car upside-down searching it and he was there for the whole morning. They had captured some *muchachos* and he went to the army headquarters asking them to please set the men free because he didn't want his arrival to be stained with blood. There was a huge crowd — all the people who were organised used to walk with him, and so it was that day. He was surrounded by all his people. They all had to run where they could or they would have been captured. If they had not been with Monseñor Romero, once outside the town they would have been captured. The delegates [of the word] were there with him: it was a serious thing to be a delegate in those days. Some were shot.

Women in the church
Pamela: Were some of the delegates women?

Doña Isabel: Yes, there were women, but most of them were men.

Pamela: In your present pastoral team, are there women?

Doña Isabel: Yes, most of them. There is one man, and a boy from the youth group, but most are women. It's like that in most places.

Pamela: Is the role of women changing? Are they realising that there should be more equality with men?

Doña Isabel: Certainly, we are fighting for that. People thought that only men could do certain things, but we women are proving that we are capable. If we have a group of women in the church, they are capable of standing up before all the people to say what they think, on the Gospel or anything. When Father Jon is not here, the women see to the celebrations.

The celebration is prepared by a team, one person does the introduction, then the choir sings, then another person, a woman, comments on the Gospel, with questions from the people, and sometimes there are dramatisations of the Gospel. The people like this because it gives them a way of expressing their understanding of the reading. But the priest is nearly always there.

Winning people over
When Jesus won his first little group, the disciples were like

people today — they couldn't serve God because they were busy with their own thing. He won them over and formed his group. That's what it's been like with the Salvadorean people, that's been the struggle — people have had to be won over.

With people who are already aware it's easy, but the struggle has been to win people who were not aware. But they weren't aware because no one had told them. That's how it was with Jesus. There was a time when his disciples even scolded him because he was eating with a sinner, Matthew. It was like that even for him — and he is the Lord. We have to win people over that we know are families of the military, and we've had to talk to them to get them to come with us.

Pamela: Have you succeeded?

Doña Isabel: Largely. Here in these parts near Chalatenango, between Chalate and here, we have been going out to 'win over' and we haven't been badly received.

Pamela: About the ending of the war. We in Britain know from our experience in the 1939-45 war that everything didn't come right at once when it was over.

Doña Isabel: That always happens. Here we never say the fight is over. The fight has begun. Because, here, all of us are poor; but in the struggle we have to see how we are going to change things so that everyone has what they need. We aren't going to be rich, but we have said at least we'll have this, that the organisation will last, and that there is unity, so that what one person says another believes. That's the struggle.

Pamela: You got results from the fast because you were organised. Because without organisation . . .

Fasting against violence

Doña Isabel took part in the 23-day fast of November 1993, based in the church, when trades union members, priests, parliamentarians, ex-combatants and representatives of FMLN organisations protested about the acts of violence, and tried to obtain firm commitments for the creation of an independent mechanism to investigate the activities of the death squads. This commission was subsequently set up and produced a report in July 1994. It concluded that structures similar to, and possibly by-products of, the death squads of the late 1970s and 1980s continued to operate within the larger context of organised crime.

Doña Isabel: Without organisation, nothing happens. There was one big team responsible for organising outside the church, that got the people together, to take them to the Commissions, and another team inside, getting out the denunciations. ONUSAL [the UN monitoring mission] supported us too, and kept a strict watch from the first day until it ended.

Pamela: Have you any message for women in our country? What would you say are the most important points in a time of violence against women?

Doña Isabel: The most important thing is to have trained groups at the level of the people; you need to train a secretariat first, a group of five or more women. They should begin to discuss how to prevent actions against women. We women have to get organised in the church and elsewhere to fight for our rights. Because sometimes we are raped even in our own homes. There is no freedom of expression because husbands think they are the ones who give the orders, and the woman can't say 'I'm going to do this' freely. So here in our department we have formed a team like that, and in addition you need a small executive. There are branches in the communities, with other women who will organise the people in the community. We've been doing this for some time, we already have groups of women in charge of training. I have two groups here of 50 women, apart from those already organised, working in small groups on some small projects. We do this so as to explain to the women how they must stand up for themselves and not give in.

Women and men together

So the news gets around. Many women are now becoming aware of their dignity, their importance, and that it shouldn't be only the men who are in control in the community and in the home. We are all equal. If there are men in the house, they should help with the women's work so that they don't feel they are more important. That's the principle we work on here.

If I teach other women, I have to be an example myself in my house. If my men don't touch a plate, take a broom to sweep, or help with the meals, I can't talk to the other women. The men have their work on the hills and in the fields, but when they can they should do their share.

A testimony from the pastoral team of Guarjila

We were refugees for six years in Mesa Grande. The community learnt to live in solidarity one with another, and we carried out some social work, like electrical installations, popular education from kindergarten to adults, health organisation in the camp, and so forth. Another important point was that we kept up the organisation we had belonged to here in El Salvador, we consolidated it.

All this was independent of the government, since the community learnt to manage itself. We learnt various skills, like shoemaking, crafts, tackle, tin work, brickmaking, vegetable gardens, carpentry, etc. We were able to organise ourselves so that we could return to our places of origin with international recognition.

From *Tiempo de Recordar y Tiempo de Contar.*
San Salvador: 'Pedro Arrupe' Jesuit Development Service, 1994.

So with the men we try to see how we can achieve all this, little by little. Women shouldn't think that because they are women they can't do anything. Of course they can. There are women here who can make a table or chair just as well as a man can. Now we have a group of six women making a vegetable garden, I think they have already begun to sell their radishes.

As we see how these things work, we'll be doing more. The women here can work, they can plant corn, beans, they have their little plots in the winter. The women don't hang back because there are men who can do the work, they work too, and the men don't get frightened, because the women do it well.

Conversation with Suyapa Guarjila, Chalatenango

Suyapa was in charge of education in the latter part of the war, and for three years was leader of all the teachers in Guarjila. She then became education representative and adviser at the Coordinating Committee of Communities and Resettlements of Chalatenango (CCR). When she left education she was given a number of different tasks — including at one point being in charge of the day nursery — and was then on the executive of the CCR. One of her responsibilities in the committee was human rights, and she was also in charge of town twinnings and inter-town relationships. On this visit we were accompanied by Carmen Broz, a Salvadorean Quaker.

Pamela: Suyapa, will you tell us how old you were when you began this work?

Suyapa: Thirteen. Now I'm 22 and I have two children.

Pamela: How was it that you began this work so young?

Suyapa: Well, for as long as I can remember I was living in an atmosphere of war, when people were organising. When I was seven everyone took part in 'happy afternoons', parties for men, women and children. There was organisation but not yet repression on a big scale. There had not yet been bombings, but a few people had disappeared. However, I was already beginning to live this, to feel it, to see the repression, so it was easy to get involved.

The white hand
Then in the municipalities all the people identified by the armed forces and the government as being organised had

the white hand put on their door.[42] Many of my relations or neighbours left their houses at six o'clock in the morning with their children and their bits and pieces, and I began to hear things. The white hand meant death, it meant, 'Either you stay a few more minutes and get killed, or you go at once'. It was a method used to frighten people off the organisations. Every organised family experienced the white hand. It was meant to make us leave our homes. When we left they ransacked the houses or burnt them. So we began to leave our homes to go to the mountains, fleeing, trying to save our lives, because we were already marked: to be organised was to be subversive, communist. Just because we wanted social change they wanted to kill us.

Bodies in the alleyway

This got worse when people began to participate in political activities in massive numbers. There were activities in San Salvador where the main streets were packed with people. Also at that time Monseñor Romero began speaking out in his Sunday homilies for respect for human rights, for an end to the repression. Day and night they took people out and in the morning bodies appeared in the alleyways. I lived through that. I saw it. So it was going to be hard for me to change. How could I say: 'The armed forces are a good thing. The ones who respect human rights are the armed forces'?

I remember — you'll laugh — but I remember when I was nine, I think, I left the house one day with one of my sisters. About 50 tanks and military trucks arrived in the municipality, Arcatao — they filled the place. I said to my sister: 'Let's go.' But we couldn't go far, we were so nervous that we couldn't walk, we imagined we felt the bullets already hitting us in the back. Then they began capturing people, getting people off the buses, ill-treating them, kicking them, and whacking them with their rifles.

---

42. Death squads painted a white hand on the door of so-called subversives as a sign that they would be 'dealt with'.

In the organisation

So we went to a place called La Cañada where about 35 families had already gone, and we stayed there. We made trenches for defence, because we thought the air force would come. There was already some education, so we began to organise more: the woman who could do something made an effort to teach the children to read. At the same time we were preparing our defences. We were a key target and they pursued us as subversives to be exterminated.

In the face of death you have to prepare to defend yourself. When I was a student they had us sharpening bamboo poles and putting them in certain places so that when the enemy came in search of us to kill us, they had a surprise. The enemy suffered many losses like this. We weren't proud of this, because they had a right to life too — we were sorry for them because they were being used, but something had to be done.

Flight to Honduras

I was aware and organised from the age of seven. I liked to take part in all the activities, political and others. Later, we had to leave in a *guinda* and go to the Honduran border. Then we were forcibly relocated in Mesa Grande, where there were 11,000 refugees, and there I trained to be a community teacher. At 13, I decided to teach the children of the camps, and Caritas[43] gave us training. I trained and then began working as a community teacher of pre-school age children.

In that year they elected me to be coordinator of the group of 12 pre-school teachers, and to be group representative. There were seven camps with a group for each one, so there had to be a coordinating group. I was in that coordinating group — there were 13 of us, and about 45 pre-school classes. It was a big task, but we had the support of a few women brought by Caritas, who were Spanish and professional teachers. We had three professional teachers

43. An international Catholic aid agency.

who directed the educational process, the materials and the training we needed. So I began to stand out as a community teacher.

Then we prepared for the return to our places of origin, which happened in 1987.

Pamela: Why did you come back in 1987, when nothing had changed here and there was great danger? I can understand that you wanted to come back to your country, but other refugees didn't return then.

Suyapa: We said: 'What are we doing in a country that isn't ours? In El Salvador there's a lot to do. Our places of origin are destroyed. We have to go back and rebuild them. We have to live in them. We have to cultivate that land, which has produced nothing for more than seven years.' Everything had been abandoned after the burnings by the enemy. So we had to come back and defend the land. The organisation and the struggle had been for that. As refugees we could do nothing — we couldn't go on fighting because we were refugees in another country: how could we make our demands to the government of Honduras? We had to come back to El Salvador, to be in our communities and to join the social movement, the people's organisations in the country, to make a greater effort. And we had to come to support the Frente (FMLN).

We prepared for a year, with meetings of all the people who were ready to come, every Saturday and Sunday. We prepared them ideologically and politically, because we had to be quite clear that we were coming back to face the same situation we had left: the country was at war, the military were the same, showing no respect, killing whoever they wanted to kill. So we had to prepare to face the same situation, and now it wasn't a question of going back, staying five days in Guarjila and then fleeing when the enemy arrived. It was a case of going back to stay in Guarjila and facing up to the enemy in any situation. And so it proved to be: military detachments came through one after the other, but we, with our consolidated organisation, stayed put in our communities until the war was over. Now we are defending our right to the land.

The CCR
For the past eight months I've been on the executive of the Coordinating Committee of Communities and Resettlements of Chalatenango (CCR). There are 16 of us, including seven women. The proportion of women to men doesn't matter if the work is effective; we get on well with the men and there are no conflicts. We need to enlarge the group because the CCR's work is vast: maintaining the coordination and the organisation in 43 communities. Among these are the resettlements of people from Mesa Grande, and communities which have organised themselves here — they were displaced within the country and they've come back — and other communities which joined the people fleeing on the mountains. There are 15 communities asking to be admitted to the CCR.

We have several sectors, so we need quite an efficient organisation. In order to be effective, the fundamental thing is programming, having a strategic plan, knowing what you want to achieve, and seeing if it fits in with the reality the people are living. Then make a plan with those who understand you and your aims, and let that plan produce another — and so on, progressively. It was like this at the beginning of the revolution here in El Salvador. First there were those who awoke and showed the way, and that helped others of us to awaken and join in the process. They went on informing us about the situation and the reality we were living, because even when you experience it in your own bones, you are sometimes incapable of perceiving it. So what is needed is a plan that is really appropriate to the place, to the field in which you are going to work.

The Christian community
We here in the organisation were helped by the pastoral teams. When the organisation began to develop, there were

quite a few delegates, celebrants of the word, including women delegates. They were mostly trained by Rutilio Grande and Monseñor Romero when he was converted.

The celebrants of the word and the parish priests organised catechists and more celebrants. They continued expanding the organisation, side by side with other peasant communal leaders who joined.

Using the Bible

The Bible has many good elements which we can use. If you know how to read the Bible and can gather the fundamentals of it for your people, that helps to awaken them. But there are also people, ultra-rightwing priests, who use the Bible to put people to sleep. The effect of the Bible is different according to who is reading it, and the interpretation given.

Really, the Bible teaches us many good things, if you study it deeply and in groups. 'What do you think of the word of God? What is it teaching us? What message has it for us?' So the people begin to comment, to dialogue – 'Is it this? Is the situation we are living what God wants?' Then they begin to wake up and say: 'No, God doesn't want a society where inequality prevails.' So people become aware of the world they live in. Sometimes poverty can be overwhelming, killing, torturing, but you are incapable of seeing it as injustice because you have been told that that is God's will. As long as you believe that it is God's will, you are trapped. 'We have to die as God wills.' That is not what God wants.

Respect for human rights

God wants respect for citizens, for universal rights, for human rights and for a whole lot of rights that we should know about in order to build that consciousness. Sometimes we think respect for human rights refers only to death. We were ignorant like this during the war — for us, the violation of human rights only meant killing. It isn't only that. The question of human rights is so wide that to defend them you have to know them. If you don't know them, you yourself allow them to be violated.

Solidarity
The other important thing is to have people who commit themselves to continuing the human support of their own brothers and sisters. It could be in a small community or a parish. Here we were helped by the existence of the church. There have been a lot of popular songs which help to combat ignorance, such as, 'When the poor believe in the poor, we can sing freedom'.

The church
Pamela: Have you felt supported by the church, strengthened by the base communities?

Suyapa: The church has always played a fundamental part with regard to the organisation. Here we have a great parish priest [Jon Cortina] who has never preached that the will of God is that we should die, that we are poor because it is God's will. The priests here are clear, aware — and they have lived through the same experience as we have. They have accompanied us, they have always been with us, and the church has always played a determining role in these communities.

But there are municipalities in El Salvador where the parish priests, if they are aware, cannot express it because the churchgoers are not aware. They would say: 'That priest is a communist; we don't want a communist Mass.' But here they are free to express themselves and they help us. All the people here are Christians, and the Mass is something that helps us a lot in not depriving us of the riches of our experience — we are always remembering what we have gone through, looking to the future, organising for the social changes that were planned in 1980. I am a Christian and the church is all right, but if there is something that doesn't seem right, I reject it. We have the right to an opinion.

The Exodus and the return

Carmen Broz: As you were speaking, I was making notes on how to build an organisation, because the First World needs to know how to organise. If you remember, the people's movement [the base] began from a religious perspective. Biblical interpretation has always been from the vision of reality. I remember when the people of El Barrillo returned to their land from the refuges of Calle Real and Domus Mariae, they themselves said: 'We are returning to the Promised Land.' They had had the Exodus, now it was the return, and Moses was leading them. I remember the night we got back to Aguacayo, which was the first Salvadorean town to be totally destroyed, the passage chosen for that night's liturgy was from Amos: 'You will go back to your destroyed lands, you will plant your gardens again, you will drink wine, use the fruit, and no one ever again will chase you out, because I, God, plant you in these lands.' It was something so real at that moment — it wasn't happening 2,000 years ago. It was a tremendous feeling that the Bible was an actual reality.

Suyapa: We had the same testimony here — the very same. We got back and the community of San José las Flores, which had already repopulated, with El Barrillo, came to greet us. When we arrived it was to a desert of tall, yellow weeds — it was summer — and full of thorns. In the afternoon there was a Mass of welcome. The Bishop came and five priests. It was a really lovely Mass. We had the same reading, about the Exodus and the Promised Land.

That was the arrival. We then began to stand up to the army and nobody got us out. So far, no one has got us out, and no one will.

Subversive memory

Pamela: Are you sure that the young today, the 10- or 12-year-olds, will continue in the same spirit, with the same degree of organisation?

Suyapa: There is a determining factor which I think will allow us to continue in the same way, and that is our history. We can't forget what we have lived through, or our loved ones. Here there is not a family unmarked by the war, with their children lost, their father disappeared, or their mother dead. Not one family. How can I forget and how can I not motivate my two children? Never. Why? Three of my brothers died, I lost my father, an aunt lost five sons in the war. What we have conquered, up to now, has been through the sacrifice of our loved ones. That can't be left as history. Cristiani [the president] should stop saying that the war is over, and that now everything is reconciliation and peace. The war of bombs and bullets is silent, but we have an inner war in our hearts which we are still living. We want peace, otherwise what will the future be, what will happen to the children who are being born?

That is why we are defending popular education as fundamental. Cristiani and some ARENA deputies are demanding that the so-called community teachers should be dismissed because they supposedly have a totally communist doctrine, from Marx, Lenin, and so on. But we are going to continue fighting: our schools come from our sacrifice. Why did the [education] ministry not show interest in us during the war? Then, they destroyed the schools, they didn't educate the children, they killed us. Now, in today's political climate, they want to take the schools back. We have a right to education, and the state has the obligation to give it, but we don't want ARENA teachers to come and change or indoctrinate our children, to change our history. That cannot be. How can we allow an eight-year-old kid, whose father was killed in the war trying to win justice and equality, to be educated with a different ideology? We cannot allow that.

We are continuing a struggle with the ministry on the basis of the peace accords on health and education. It is not moving ahead much because the people from the ministry are very slow, focusing on political points and not the needs of the people. We are demanding the accreditation of community teachers who have 12 years' experience. I was nine years in popular education, I am qualified for pre-school, and I can tell you that a teacher with a degree or diploma can't do better than me. I have the experience, I have been with the children all the time, in every circumstance. We are fighting for equal salaries, but it hasn't happened yet.

The Salvadorean Women's Movement

Isabel de Guevara was director of the Salvadorean Women's Movement (MSM). Founded on 25 February 1988 as a coalition of urban and rural committees and organisations, the MSM was a response to the need of women's groups for a national dimension. By the end of 1988 it was fairly well known. An autonomous organisation (that is, not linked to any political or church institution), it works for gender equality and social justice. An MSM leaflet says: 'We identify principally with women at the base [*las mujeres del pueblo*], with whom we work for the building of a new society where peace rules over violence, justice over inequalities, development over poverty, and respect for differences over discrimination.' The movement's objectives are: to promote gender equality in communities, social organisations and political parties; and to initiate and carry out training and education, social services and production projects for women. The MSM is established in 32 municipalities in nine of the country's departments, and belongs to various coordinating bodies of women's organisations, including Mujeres '94 and the Coordination of Women's Organisations (COM).

The MSM went through difficult times in 1989, especially after the FMLN offensive which began in November. Many women were captured and tortured. Isabel herself and her husband and children had to leave the country and go to the United States. They returned in 1993, by which time the situation had eased following the signing of the peace accords in Mexico in January 1992.

In May 1994 the premises shared by the MSM and the Madeleine Lagadec Centre for the Promotion of Human Rights (see next chapter) were searched and ransacked and the security guard was shot dead outside the building. The MSM denounced the incident as an attempt to frighten the

137

women and deprive them of their hard-won right to exist as a social movement.

Isabel told us that, although women were participating more, were more aware and clearer about what they wanted, there was still a strong feeling that a woman's place was in the home. Work had to be done to help them value themselves and have confidence in their ability to accomplish work other than domestic.

Isabel de Guevara: We want a government which will listen to us as women, as *pueblo*. But they only listen to the rich, to the 14 families. Reconciliation between the government and FMLN is difficult — the images implanted by the government have hardened in people's minds.

But now that the FMLN and the government have been negotiating, embracing each other — how can the people go on hating each other? There is a process towards friendship.

Sadly, in the months following our visit, much happened to weaken that process and to put in question the good faith of both sides regarding the agenda of the impoverished majority.

Dolores
A valiant woman

We met Dolores in the offices of the Madeleine Lagadec Human Rights Centre. She was 54 at the time.

Dolores' husband had been killed in the war in 1980, leaving her with eight children. After her husband's death she worked at a variety of tasks, from making and selling *tortillas* to representing families of the disappeared, helping them to find out what happened to their family members. She also worked with orphans, with refugees in Zacamil (a neighbourhood on the west of the capital), collecting clothes for them, and with political prisoners in Mariona jail, taking food in for them and taking out their protests. She worked for a time with the parish priests in Zacamil.

At one point she formed a widows' group and went from house to house after Mass, doing bible commentaries. A son of 17 and a daughter of 20 were captured, and she herself had to leave the country. She went to Nicaragua where she joined the Salvadorean Women's Movement (MSM) and produced its newsletters.

After the victory of the rightwing United National Opposition Party (UNO) in Nicaragua in 1990 Dolores went to Cuba, where she joined other Salvadoreans and worked for a time in a camp for the wounded. While in Cuba the strain of all she had been through took its toll and she became ill. She was well looked after in hospital and was able to begin working with orphaned Salvadorean children in Cuba. It was her task to explain to the children why their parents were not with them — breaking the news that they were dead, or explaining that for their safety they had sent the children out of El Salvador.

Dolores's son, Pedro Antonio, was the guerrilla leader Camilo Turcios. He was killed in San Vicente in 1991, one of three of Dolores's sons killed in the war. Pedro Antonio had been her one support, and his death made her ill again. She remembered how he used to tell her to be strong, and not to cry when he was killed. She prayed to Mary for help at this time.

The Madeleine Lagadec Human Rights Centre

Dolores returned to El Salvador after the signing of the peace accords in January 1992, and began work at the Centro Madeleine Lagadec. Founded in 1992, the centre is named after a French nurse killed in San Vicente in 1989 by a unit of the Salvadorean Air Force. It bombed the FMLN mobile hospital where she was working, killing five of the 15 people working there. The focus of the centre's work is support for rural communities. Using its network of 58 regional and local promoters, the centre has run campaigns on the right to vote, violence against women, human rights, and the implementation of the recommendations of the truth commission set up under the peace accords. For the 1994 elections, the centre concentrated on a voter-education campaign.

Dear Guerrilla: Camilo Turcios

In many ways Camilo was a typical peasant: suspicious at first, observant and cautious; little by little we began to work together and from the first I was surprised by the great gift he had for listening to others. He always asked for their opinions which he jotted down in a little exercise book, which he later often lost because he was very untidy, or on bits of paper which he put in his trousers pockets or anywhere, but he always noted and remembered the opinions of others, and this helped him in his decisions. [After he was killed] I understood that the death of Camilo was an irreparable loss [...] I remembered a phrase or thought that sums up his life and his death quite well: I thought that Camilo who had always gone about with his heart open, ended when the last drop of his blood had ebbed out of it.

From Mario Ramos, *Querido Guerrillero — Al año de la muerte de Camilo Turcios*
(undated, privately printed)

Dolores got permission from the authorities to exhume her son and his partner. The newspaper *Diario Latino* of 11 July 1994 reported on a ceremony in the town of Santa Clara in the Department of San Vicente: a mural had been unveiled marking a tomb with bodies of fallen guerrilla leaders, among them Pedro Antonio, Comandante Camilo. Dolores was there.

The Madeleine Lagadec Centre has exhumed 30 bodies and buried them in the Santa Clara cemetery, and the work continues. On 7 March 1995, *The Guardian* newspaper carried a picture of a group of Salvadoreans coming away from an exhumation, carrying the remains of their relatives in cardboard boxes. Work is also continuing to find children who disappeared during the war, many of whom had been taken by the military and put into refuges. (See note on Asociación Pro-Búsqueda de los Niños, page 111)

In May 1994 the premises of the centre and the MSM were ransacked and the security guard murdered, prompting the centre to publish a leaflet setting out the principles of their work for human rights and asking: 'Will the promotion of human rights continue to be a motive for persecution in this country?'

The day before we left El Salvador, we met Dolores by chance at the Central American University — she had with her a copy of *Querido Guerrillero* [Dear Guerrilla] and we photographed her holding it against her heart.

There are many valiant women in El Salvador, and Dolores, with her quiet strength, belongs with the best of them.

Isabel Ascencio

We met Isabel in the busy office of the Regional Committee of the Sixth Latin American and Caribbean Feminist Encounter. Isabel had been a pastor in the Lutheran Church in El Salvador, and had left this church for reasons which she did not disclose to us.

She had attended the first regional meeting of women in Central America which took place in Managua, Nicaragua, in 1992, and in a published interview on her return summed up the new spirit moving women in El Salvador:

> In El Salvador we are trying to build a broad-based women's movement which will respond to the needs and problems of women. We don't want to build a new society with the same patriarchal values that we have now. We want the new society to reflect the values for which women have heroically struggled during these past 12 years of war, both in the FMLN and the popular movement. Otherwise we will simply repeat the same patriarchal scheme.

She went on to speak of women's commitment to work for independence:

> The women's movement still has to struggle to gain acceptance, even from our *compañeros* in the popular movement and the FMLN, many of whom still have a false conception of feminism. We are struggling to build a new kind of power and autonomy, in the sense that we want to make decisions as women, without having to ask for approval from the FMLN, from the UNTS

[National Union of Salvadorean Workers] or from
anybody [...] One of the great challenges we face
today is to enter into a dialogue with the FMLN,
with the popular movement, so that we can begin
to reflect on the demands of women, particularly
women with both gender and class consciousness.
We are looking at all of these emerging expressions of women as actors in civil society, and
working so that our demands are taken into
account during this period of reconstruction.[44]

Keeping hope alive

Pamela: Tell me about the meeting you went to yesterday.

Isabel: It was the monthly meeting of different organisations linked with the base Christian communities, Catholics
and Protestants and a new group, the independent
Christians.

Pamela: Are they people who don't belong to any church?

Isabel: Yes, people who for one reason or another don't
work within any church but are 'doing theology' at some
level. It is very important to recognise this new way of
expressing one's faith, because in this country people are
often valued or recognised according to what organisation
they represent, or even how many people they represent.
Women here are breaking down that attitude and saying
that people can also just represent themselves. So here,
within the 'open space' of the base communities, we have
achieved the participation of Catholics, Protestants and
independent Christians.

The aim of this meeting was to celebrate and reflect on
the word of God and also to evaluate the work we have
been doing — what mistakes we've made, what we have
achieved, and so on. We also had our first chance to discuss

44. Isabel Ascencio, 'Women Challenging the Revolution in Central America', in
Challenge, Vol 3, No 1, Spring 1992. Washington DC: EPICA.

the big issues which came up at a recent national forum of church representatives and see how we might carry them forward. One of the things this Christian movement does is to have a monthly celebration to remember the martyrs and recognise the testimony of their lives. Their example helps us to renew our strength and give each other courage. We also spend an hour analysing the situation in the country with the help of a knowledgeable speaker. Yesterday the speaker was from the political commission of the FMLN.

The most important thing is how to keep hope alive, how to become strong through working in the community. These are things that give me, at least, a lot of hope and courage. The methodology we use aims to involve everyone. All have responsibilities connected with the workshops and this creates a joyful atmosphere because everybody knows they are participating — they have a role to play in planning, organising and evaluating the meeting.

We have been able to break away from the sectarianism which was characteristic of the war years. During the war it was natural, because we had many traitors and you needed to take care of yourself. There was a lot of tension between the five political parties of the FMLN which each had their own zones of control. Everything was clandestine. Many Christians took a political and military stand on the basis of their faith, and this gave them strength and motivation, but we had people from the north of Chalatenango who did not want to meet with people from the north of Morazán, and political affiliations preventing churches in San Salvador from working together. These things are now very difficult to change, but the 'open space' broke through this sectarianism and we have been meeting together now for nearly three years, sharing our experiences of life with faith.

'They want autonomy'

Pamela: Do you think the politicians are changing their values and their language along the same lines?

Isabel: The structure of the political parties, the churches and even the popular organisations is so vertical, so hierarchical, that the human beings inside the structure are not able to develop. It creates images, idols, leaders whom one has to follow. People wait for a word from their leaders, for the party line.

It used to be the normal thing for us to see what was the party line to follow, but if your work for any reason led you to do something else, then you were not following the party line any more. You became someone who was against the line, like an enemy, or people would just tell you: 'We don't need you any more.' During a time of war it is necessary to follow the line — it is a valuable and justifiable thing to do for security reasons.

I think we women were the first to rebel against this style of exercising power, each of us in our own situation. Then we started to share our rebelliousness and to discover that the way in which the system is organised, including the trade unions, the political parties and the church, is not helping our development or giving us strength for the things we want to do. Then some people were expelled from their party, or they lost their jobs.

A lot of people left and became independent. They want to be called 'independent', which is a way of saying: 'I am not feeling represented in this style of organisation, but I want to be a part of what is going on and here I am.' As Christians or as feminists, these independent women participate in many activities and take on responsibilities but, as we say here: 'They represent their own tapeworms', not any organisation. They want autonomy.

The FMLN representative yesterday talked about autonomy too. He was complaining that civil society is expecting the FMLN to perform miracles and give them land, jobs, health care and all the things they have been waiting for. But the FMLN says it does not have a magic wand and civil society must develop some autonomy to deal with these things. But we think that one reason civil society has not been able to develop is the way it has been kept in subjection. We ourselves, as part of the women's movement, have suffered many painful experiences just because we started to think about our autonomy. They are telling us that we need to consider 'autonomy' as the solution to our problems, but when we start to put this into practice . . .

Pamela: They don't like it.

Isabel: They say: 'Wait a minute. What sort of autonomy is that? Where do you women think you are going?' So I believe we are now in a transitional moment, redefining our ways of working, because people are tired of this vertical and hierarchical style of power. When people participate in the planning and organisation of the work they feel happy and fulfilled, but if you are only taking orders, and the result of the work is not what you expected, then you feel frustrated.

Pamela: Another important theme for us is the development of a popular theology done in a language that people can understand, and also a political language relevant to the grassroots. Do you agree?

Isabel: Yes. In this country we have several teams working on it. For instance, the Maize Team [see box opposite] which organises workshops based on the people's experience and knowledge. They work by collecting all these experiences in books that are easy to read. For instance, they write about the plan of salvation, using real names and situations, even the names of well-known foods. This is a useful method because a large proportion of our population does not know how to read or write. We need to use visual aids to start us off and then progress from there. We start with the real situation, with familiar symbols at the beginning, and then go on to create our own. There is a great need for us women to create our own symbols.

We need to keep walking along together in order to learn more. The base Christian communities used to have

---

The Maize Education Team

The Equipo de Educación Maíz (Maize Education Team) published in 1994 a selection from the homilies of Archbishop Oscar Romero, with photographs and graphics. *Monseñor Romero. The People is my Prophet* is meant to be a sort of catechism of Monseñor Romero, a tool for pastoral workers, a source for bible study groups and the celebrations of the word. The book's introduction says:

> To commemorate Monseñor Romero is to remember his word, and above all, to continue his work, promoting what he called liberating evangelisation, being a prophetic people, following Jesus as he did with radicality and sincerity.

On the cover we read:

> We haven't published [the book] to remember the past, but to face the present and the future with clarity and hope.

People's Schools of Theology, but they have been wiped out. Many illiterate people went to them and came out understanding their responsibilities and level of political participation. From there they went on to other levels of political participation. But when the work of those schools became known, they suffered the most terrible massacres. The areas where the schools worked were razed to the ground and many priests, nuns and lay men and women were killed. Because this was a seed which bore fruit, some people felt it necessary to destroy those ideas. It was the same with the murder of the Jesuits. They were the 'brains' so they became the focus for destruction. A theology which is going to bring about change is a dangerous thing that some people cannot accept. This explains the persecution we have suffered in Latin America.

We think that now it is necessary for us to change the way we work. At the moment there is a strong growth of conservative church movements in the towns and small communities. These are the 'charismatics', the conservative elements of the Catholic church such as Opus Dei, and the conservative evangelical sects. Their approach appeals directly to people's hearts. It makes them feel valued and that they have a piece of work to do. They use psychological pressures but they give people a feeling of belonging.

On the other side we have the base communities giving a very high profile to political participation. People feel terrified of war and massacres so they don't want to hear anything about politics. They have heard that every time a town was massacred, only the members of the Pentecostal church escaped. Members of the Pentecostal church did not need to be afraid, but if someone had a picture of Monseñor Romero or Father Rutilio Grande, they disappeared. People remember these experiences. So what we need is to start with people's needs and talk to them more. Also we must walk at the right pace and not fall into despair because people do not understand that the problem is nothing to do with the other world. For them, the problem is the other world and that is what they are looking for. We think we must have more patience about these things and understand where people are coming from.

We also have the challenge of keeping hope alive, reflecting together in order to interpret the moments we are living through by discerning the signs of the times. We need to explain this moment of transition and see that there are perfectly good explanations for people's unhappiness. We need to talk more about democracy and how to build it, and also to stress how much we can gain from it, because if there is nothing to gain we don't become enthusiastic about it and democracy becomes just another word, another flag to wave.

We talked about all these things in the forum we had. I find it very moving when someone comes and says: 'I started in the school of Los Naranjos', which was a school for peasants, 'and then I became a preacher of the word. I studied the Bible and understood what was happening around me, and became an active member of the FMLN. But now I am asking myself questions, especially about how power is being used. We did things in a certain way because there was a war on, but now it is different. We have other possibilities.' This is a process of being engaged with reality on the basis of our faith.

The Sects: Autonomous religious groups

The attitude of the Latin American church to the sects is not usually one of confrontation or of distance, because the sects are not a problem, but a response to a problem. The sects respond in their own way to a search for meaning, for the sacred, for God. It is true that we can criticise their methods (seduction, psychological pressure, charlatanism, economic exploitation, etc), but we cannot judge them primarily on this superficial level. The deeper level is that they respond to the search for God, for personal identity, for meaning.

In my parish in Rio de Janeiro there are seven *favelas* where I work, and I have noticed that when a family from a *favela* becomes a member of a sect, they acquire a sense of dignity. They feel special, chosen, and they begin to feel good, they begin to work, to organise their family life. They feel important, they have a function in their church community, and they even improve their material life. They look you in the face, their eyes meet yours, and they no longer feel humiliated. I thank God for this, for the good work done by these sects among these poor people. [...]

Fr José Comblin, a Belgian theologian who spent many years in Latin America, warned that because of the mistake the church is making with regard to the sects, in one hundred years from now Latin America will be one great Pentecostal continent, no longer Catholic, although today it is the only great Catholic continent in the world. He says we need to study how the sects respond to people's hunger. We need to devise the kind of flexible, effective methods that they use. The Catholic church is weighed down by a heavy weight of structures, both on the doctrinal and organisational levels. It is too centralised.

From Clodovis Boff OSM, 'The Church in Latin America: Between perplexity and creativity' in *SEDOS Bulletin*, 1995.

Pamela: Yes, because that is an engagement which can be kept whatever the circumstances, and which never dies. Has the theology of liberation influenced the women's movement?

Isabel: Yes. In the beginning the theology of liberation influenced us by making us aware of our social and class situation. We became aware of ourselves as oppressed men and women. This gave us a lot of strength. We started to ask if it is natural for some people to be intelligent or stupid, rich or poor. Liberation theology became a project of the poor but it did not wake us up as women because we were just part of 'the people'. We took on responsibilities without becoming aware that we had three full-time jobs to do: work outside the home, housework, and our commitment as activists. We did not see that. We were so tired. We couldn't take part in the executive council because we didn't know how to read or write. But we did not understand why.

It was the feminist movement that shook us up as women because it helped us to ask questions. Is it because I'm a woman that I'm living in this situation? Is it because I'm a woman that I can't be at the same level as my brother? If I am a girl, they give me dolls and kitchen tools as toys. If I am a boy, I need to lead, to manage and to give orders. That is gender conditioning.

Feminist theology gave a 90 degree turn to our lives and actions. A personal challenge for me is to be part of the movement of the popular church, starting with awareness of gender conditioning, and questioning how power is used in the Christian base communities. For instance, we still have a relationship of dependency with the priests or sisters. They are very progressive, but there is always dependency. The challenge is for lay men and women to take control of their lives and go forward together. I have tried to talk about these things on a few occasions, but I found sisters who told me: 'But Isabel, I don't have a problem here; I am a man and a woman. I am everything.'

There are women who say: 'If the priest said that it is a sin, then abortion is a sin.' But they don't discuss it themselves, they don't say: 'Look, this is my opinion, now tell me what you think.'

Pamela: They are just receiving a doctrine.

Isabel: There is a great challenge here. We need an analysis of this gender conditioning. Our theological circle is making an effort through the Christian Women's Initiative (IMC). They have already managed to get it into the communities and parishes, through social projects, of course, because there is no other way. But they have managed in this project to carry out a gender-based reflection with women. They read the Gospels, the Scriptures, and reflect from the standpoint of their own situation as women. We don't see that happening in the base Christian communities. Yes, there is an understanding that women have a difficult time and need to be encouraged in their work, but that is as far as it goes. There is a clear consciousness about class oppression and the category of the poor, but not about womanhood and about the role of men in this situation. We keep on working to see how things will be in the years to come.

Pamela: In Europe we are also struggling as women. I think it is very important to feel the solidarity of women from different parts of the world. The methodology may be

---

Enrique Dussel said that in moments of historic disillusion, when the 'scientific' hope has been defeated by the facts, the Christian hope may remain alive in the light of the faith that lies beyond the scientific truths.

From José María Vigil and Pedro Casaldáliga,
'Solidarity in Crisis: A reflection on the spiritual reality of
solidarity in Latin America' in SEDOS Bulletin, 1995.

different but we have the same objective. Women have a tremendous potential for transformation. If, as women, we can find our roles and develop them, then we will have the power to transform society and the church. Do you believe that?

Isabel: Yes, of course, although I am seeing the church more and more as blocking women.

Pamela: Here, or in general?

Isabel: Here, at least, in our experience in Latin America. For instance, during the Sixth Feminist Encounter we had the opportunity to get together and hold a Feminist Theology Workshop to discuss how we are feeling as women in the church. The point is, if as women we take on the roles that the church gives us, then we don't have any problems. For instance, roles such as 'the mother', or 'the bible school teacher' or any role with children. The problems come if we reject those roles and start asking the church questions like 'Who are the people deciding these roles?' or questions about the church's projects, or even 'Who is administering the money?' If you start to question these things then you find yourself in confrontation with the church. Many women have suffered this. Some of them are still working in religious institutions, in churches, but others could not stay in them any longer. The atmosphere was suffocating.

I think this is a moment of rebellion for women. Look back in history at what happened to women who rebelled! They were burnt by the institution or accused of being mad. But we never had an organised women's movement in the church made up of conscientised women. This is a battle we have never had before. The first stage is individual rebellion; the second is to come together as women with our own rebellion, to start to question things.

Mercedes Cañas
Centre for Feminist Studies

Mercedes Cañas's acute social conscience was formed and nurtured in her family, especially by her mother, who belonged to a base Christian community and passed on to her children her commitment to bible reflection and liberation. In her early teens Mercedes became a catechist, working to bring other young people to an understanding of the gospel message of liberation. The murder of Father Rafael Palacios in Santa Tecla by the security forces in 1979, when she was 15, strengthened her commitment, although she admits she had 'not much capacity to discern reality', and began to think that 'by changing society you would also change human beings, as if one thing came first and then the other. I had seen it in the revolutionary process because it was a common focus for discussion.'

The murder of Archbishop Romero in 1980 further confirmed her and her family in the struggle for social justice, 'the building of God's kingdom'.

Later, disillusionment with the church and with popular organisations led her to feminism, which she saw as a movement which touched the root of oppression and subordination, and confirmed her belief that it was possible to change the world.

Ideas to live by
Pamela: Mercedes, will you tell us about how you came to feminism through your commitment to the revolutionary process?

Mercedes Cañas: I became politically aware through the feelings that poverty and political oppression produced in me. Those were the two things that were basic in my commitment to the revolutionary process. Likewise, in

153

making me a feminist, the basic thing was realising the violence done to women. Violence against women in this country has characteristics similar to the violence against political prisoners, against revolutionary leaders or political opponents.

So I did my university degree thesis on intra-family violence, another aspect of violence which no political theory had revealed to me. I had studied Marxism, class analysis, many faces of violence in society, but not even the most lucid theory had made me aware of family violence. In doing my thesis I studied close up the horrible face of domestic violence, which for me is one of the roots of other forms of violence. Then, as my mind opened up, I decided that feminism, for me, is the theory that is most fertile for the transformation of the world. It questions not only one form of oppression but all forms, not just one form of violence, but all forms. It is not only for liberty for all citizens, but for the individual liberty of every woman who must take her life into her own hands. So when I became a feminist, it was really like a conversion — pretty total — because it made me see that to make a different world you also need things I had begun to forget about in the [revolutionary] process: that each person is truly unique.

In feminism I began to recover the meaning of many things — a deeper sense of values and the knowledge that one can't really be a revolutionary unless one has profoundly changed one's life. One lives certain values, and only in that way can one build something better. That is something that attracts me to feminism: it is a super-radical theory. But I think that as a movement it is capable of falling into the same trap that all revolutionaries and all revolutions fall into. All types of feminism can, in the pursuit of their political objectives, forget and betray their methods, their daily practice, their relationships. However, I think that the theory at least makes us constantly review ourselves and our relationships with other women, with our families, our children, our community.

Feminism has been a transcendental discovery in my

life. It has reconciled me to many values more than a strictly political dynamic would have done, because feminism, for me, is not only in what is political but in what is spiritual. It is a proposal not only for a new social organisation, but for new values and a new way of being and a new spirituality. In a time of war, amidst political activism, there are things that are hard to keep in mind. In the midst of bullets, deaths and massacres, one sometimes loses sight of the great utopia, one only sees what is happening around one day by day.

Birth of the Centre for Feminist Studies
In 1988 Mercedes was one of a group of women who began a study circle under the auspices of the United Nations Children's Fund (UNICEF). Later, after some training, the group began to share with other women some of the ideas which had changed their lives — as Mercedes says, 'I have needed ideas to live by' — and training sessions with other women developed from this, still under the auspices of UNICEF. In 1990 the group cut off their relationship with the United Nations in order to develop their own identity, and became independent.

Desatanising feminism
Mercedes: There was a lot of argument over what to call ourselves, and in the end we chose the name the Centre for Feminist Studies. We are the only group that in its name claims feminism as a political alternative for women.

We took this name in a society where feminism is somewhat satanised, where still for the majority of people feminism equals loose living, equals lesbianism, equals destruction of the home. Nevertheless, we thought it was important to begin to desatanise feminism, and we began to move into feminist studies in 1990. We still offered training services.

We have two main lines of activity: one is feminist activism (militancy, as we call it), the political work of the Centre, done in conjunction with the whole women's movement. Our political activism lies within the Coordination of Women for Peace, Dignity and Equality. We collaborate with various organisations, and within this area of our work the fundamental objective is to contribute to the unity of the women's movement, to help promote sisterhood among women.

Our other main line of action has been training. We offer to the community, to society, a series of themes which we consider are the basic subjects needed for a critique of the system of patriarchy, male domination, *machismo*. We offer all the groups or associations which seek our services the exploration of themes, either in workshops, or talks, or seminars, according to how much time they give us and the kind of audience which will be listening. This is how we generate the dynamics, the method. These have been the two main areas of work.

Feminist Encounter
The Sixth Latin American and Caribbean Feminist Encounter took place in El Salvador in November 1993. About 1,000 women attended as representatives of women's organisations from every part of the continent, and the debate ranged over the advances and setbacks of the women's movement, especially its challenge to *machismo*.

Pamela: Mercedes, was the Centre involved in this Encounter?

Mercedes: Yes, I was a member of the regional committee which prepared the Encounter, which gave us a lot to think about. Afterwards we set ourselves new challenges, among them the challenge of a feminist analysis. Some of us had been doing some kind of feminist analysis, but not as a group — it was part of our own professional work. So now we have started doing it as a group.

At the Encounter we realised that in Central America there is a very lively feminist movement which has various expressions, not just one. There are different kinds of feminism in El Salvador — at least, that's how I see it — and in the Centre we have felt the need to systematise all this because we think there is a very rich discussion around themes such as power and the feminisation of poverty in Central America. We feel these themes have to be brought out into the open.

We are just 15 women. We don't intend to be a base [grassroots] organisation because this is not our vocation. We offer a service to organisations which have a 'base'. But we think it is questionable to talk about women of the base, because to talk about the base always means talking about hierarchy. In the case of the feminist movement, it means talking about other women who are not the base, who are in the leadership or élite or intellectuals, or any other category which is not the base. So we are not interested in generating a structure of our own with a hierarchy. Similarly, it is part of Salvadorean culture and history to talk of the 'masses', but we want the opposite — we want a change in all these patriarchal categories and language.

We want to have characteristics which will give us a more horizontal structure among ourselves. We question the use of structures which establish hierarchies, in relationships between women or any people. In fact I think, and the Centre thinks, that one of the great utopias of feminism is a society without hierarchies. This does not mean a society where everyone is the same. We know that differences enrich but we are for horizontal relationships where we can see each other as equals.

By comparison with women from 'the base', we in the Centre are not among the poorest people in El Salvador. As a group we have almost all had access to education, which in this country is a privilege: most women in El Salvador are illiterate. So what unites us is the desire that our lives may contribute to transforming the lives of women, because we know that transforming the lives of women is to transform the world and to make a truly democratic El Salvador.

<u>Political activism</u>
Pamela: What about your political activity?

Mercedes: Some of us in the Centre have a background of activism in other fields, political ones. Personally I was active on the left in the Revolutionary Party of Central American Workers (PRTC). However, although it claimed to be a revolutionary party, struggling against oppression, against the lack of liberty, in its own structure and discourse it used other forms of oppression, such as the oppression of women. One of the reasons I left the party — in fact they really pushed me out — was that I was a feminist. They decided I was no longer following the party line but the feminist line. That doesn't interest me. What interests me is to make clear that feminism extends the meaning of the word democracy, of the word oppression, of the word liberty, and in this sense enriches humanity and helps to make its structures deeper.

<u>The way of non-violence</u>
Marigold: Has there been any attempt to promote non-violent methods of struggle?

Mercedes: There came a time in our society when things became so polarised that violence was the option, armed struggle. Then peace was agreed with no solutions to the problems that produced the war. There is an intention not to go back to war, but I think there has been no deep discussion about why not go back to war, why not violence, why other forms of struggle.

In the women's movement we don't want to use violent methods because a lot of our effort is directed against violence against women, and towards denouncing violence, and seeking and carrying out solutions. In this country for some years there has been a clinic to care for battered women in the community, victims of intra-family violence, sexual violation and incest. We have done a lot of training around these themes from the beginning.

Last year it was important that the Office of the Procurator for the Defence of Human Rights, created within the peace accords, also denounced violence against women. So much of our work is concerned with the struggle against violence and we have, for example, proposed to the new National Civil Police (PNC), which was a fruit of the accords, the creation of women's commissions against violence. We have offered our services as trainers to the PNC, to sensitise them and to train them in dealing with women victims of violence. We have not received any positive response, but we have generated proposals towards the eradication of violence.

For several years we have celebrated 25 November as the Day of Non-violence Against Women. Nevertheless, we still lack discussion about what methods we should, or can,

---

Proposed legislation on domestic violence

In the early 1990s the office of the Procurator for the Defence of Human Rights in El Salvador proposed legislation against domestic violence, which it described as 'a complex phenomenon which has been invisible and which makes possible the impunity of the perpetrator and the defencelessness of the victim'. The principles governing the proposed legislation are set out as follows:

a. respect for the dignity of the person
b. equal rights of men and women
c. the right to a life with dignity and free of violence in every context, public and private
d. the protection of the family and each one of its members.

With Resolution 1994/45 the UN Commission on Human Rights decided to appoint a Special Rapporteur on Violence against Women for a period of three years. The commission also called for efforts to integrate women's rights into the human rights mechanisms of the United Nations. Radhika Coomaraswamy, the Director of the International Centre for Ethnic Studies in Sri Lanka, was appointed Special Rapporteur on Violence against Women.

---

use to contribute to building a culture of peace, a culture of democracy, which will produce personalities who exemplify peace and democracy. We're involved in a process which at times moves very quickly: what the

Women's needs

Neither the peace accords nor the final draft of the PRN [National Reconstruction Programme] deal specifically with the needs of the women. None of the programmes [...] is designed specifically for women, or tackles the problem of training for women. These and other omissions could have been overcome if the reinsertion programmes [programmes for reintegrating former combatants into society] had allowed observations by women to be incorporated. But such a process did not exist.

A woman in Nuevo Gualcho tells how she spends her day:

I get up every day at 4.30 am when it is still dark. I go to the river to wash clothes and household cloths. I wash the maize and put it on the fire before I go, so that it can soften. When I get back from the river the sun has come out; I begin to grind the maize to make *tortillas* and cook the meal. It's a load of work.

When we have a plot of land, I help my partner to clean it. We used to have water from the tap, but the pipe broke and now I have to go four times a day to the farm or to Los Mangos to bring water. Each journey is about an hour - just the journey, without counting the time you lose waiting in line. I wash the clothes in the river near here, but I have to carry the drinking water.

Juan is my only son, the other four are my sister Elba's. She works in the city of Usulután, she only comes home at weekends. My mother and I look after the children, because my sister hasn't got a partner. The father of the bigger children was killed during the war, and the other man left her with the small ones. In these days it's better not to have a lot of children, that's why I only have one.

From *Hemisphere Initiatives. Ex-Combatant Women in Nuevo Gualcho.*

women's movement in El Salvador has done has been achieved in a short time. The movement began in the mid 1970s. Many organisations were struggling for their rights even during the war and there were problems with the left itself on this account. We can't deny all that history. The National Coordination of Salvadorean Women clinic for victims of rape opened in 1990.

The women's movement has grown faster since the peace accords, especially because we analysed the peace accords and the national reconstruction plans (PRN) proposed by the government and the FMLN. It was a terrible blow to women to realise that neither the government nor the FMLN cared about women. They didn't even remember us. The reconstruction plans ignored women, the peace accords only mention us in the context of the PNC, calling on us to become policewomen. That's why, since the accords, the movement has grown so much. Things are moving very fast, so fast that sometimes we don't have time to reflect.

The feminisation of poverty

Mercedes was one of an investigative team which produced a report called *Gender Analysis in Development Projects*.[45] This reveals a situation which can only be described as the feminisation of poverty. Women make up over 50 per cent of the total population of El Salvador, one of the poorest countries in Central America. Those most affected in times of crisis are women. The data in the report not only supports the concept of the feminisation of poverty, it also underlines the social subordination of women, who do not have the same access to resources, wealth and power as men (see box, page 162). We asked Mercedes to give us her personal impressions of the lives of women in El Salvador.

Mercedes: We are investigating the conditions of life of women in the department of Morazán, and it has been

---

45. *Análisis de Género en Proyectos de Desarrollo*. Technofem/PRODERE, El Salvador, 1992.

Work and employment
Women make up only 34.9 per cent of the work force, 65.1 per cent being made up by men. Domestic work undertaken by women in their families is not considered work so is not included in the statistics.

Employment figures (per cent)

	Women	Men
Employed	25.3	35.2
Underemployed	68.1	60.1
Unemployed	6.6	4.7

A survey carried out in 1992 concluded that domestic work and the care of children was the exclusive responsibility of the women, who work 16-18 hours a day, getting up between 4 and 5 am and going to bed between 8 and 10 pm, without respite and without any kind of holiday. Among the daily tasks of the women are:

• grinding the corn and making *tortillas* three times a day
• making the coffee and food to go with it three times a day
• feeding the animals at least twice a day
• going shopping daily or weekly.

shattering to see how they live. Most of them have no income, no income. We're trying to find out how they survive.

Most families sow even a tiny bit of land; some sow on borrowed land on condition they give half the crop to the owner. Then, in order to have a little money for salt and soap (which are almost the only things they buy), they sell a little bit of maize. We have found communities that were a 'base' for the FMLN, north of the Torola river. We've been there, and in Arambala and Segundo Montes, in fact in the whole department, and the people there are worse off than before the war. Before, they had a house of adobe, now they have a house of maize stalks.

Pamela: In Segundo Montes?

Mercedes: No, not Segundo Montes — but you've seen in Segundo Montes those nice houses that cost 11,000 *colones*. How can they get the money for a house like that if they don't even earn one *colón* a day? Those houses are only accessible to a few people who are not from the base, people who are employed by one of the non-governmental organisations (NGOs) there. We have talked to the women and they are in despair: they are worn down by poverty and they have no alternatives. They will say to you: I'd like to have some work which would give me even 10 *centavos* a day. They have no access to money, nothing. Nothing to buy salt with. You ask them what their problems are and they can't tell you because everything is a problem for them. They say, from salt upwards, everything is a problem for me. It's misery.

We've been to some places where it's like going back to the time of cave people. You find women sitting on a stone, with another stone in their hand, crushing olive stones one by one. Women of 26 who already have five children, without a single tooth in their head. And who cares about these women? No one. Sometimes not even we feminists who are here putting on political activities and fora. What are we doing for these women? No one is interested because they are marginalised from everything.

Pamela: What about the future?

Mercedes: That's what I ask myself too. The future is those of us who can see these things and give some response to the situation — responses which transform this reality and don't just patch it up.

The international organisations (for which I've been evaluating projects) say they are doing development projects with these communities. For instance, in a development project in Chalatenango they have given 10 cows to 10 women. Those cows give 12 bottles of milk a day. Some days they sell the milk at 1 *colón* a bottle — 12 pathetic *colones*, and they are 10 women. On some days they share the milk between them. In order to care for these cows, these 10 women have to get up very early and walk for an hour. Some of them are pregnant, because these women have no access to information on birth control, and in any case they have been filled with myths by the church about how bad it is. So they get up early to milk the cows, and in the evening they go off again to find the cows and tether them. All this work to have a tiny bit of milk, because the money they earn is only enough to buy the vaccine for the cows or the medicines for them. They don't earn anything, their life doesn't change in the slightest. All they have is a little more food, and often they don't eat it themselves but give it to their children who, they say, need it more. And those are the UN development projects. The lives of those women don't change; all they get is more work. The UN is so irresponsible that it doesn't give enough training to the women.

If we really want to make a different future, we have to invest, but in a really responsible way, which truly seeks to change the conditions of life for these women.

Pamela: Is popular education where we have to begin? Training?

Mercedes: I think various things have to happen simultaneously. We have to give work to these women that really gives them an income, some dignity. So we need real development projects which give them access to the resources to improve their life. We must give a lot of education — formal education, and education in reproductive rights and birth control. It is terrible how women die from going on and on having children at the risk of their own lives. We must generate services that reduce their daily workload a bit. Now women have to spend hours getting water in a country where it would not be difficult to get water to all parts. It is a tiny country, there are roads everywhere. It wouldn't be hard if anyone cared about it. We must also generate services such as day care centres for children.

Most of the women give birth not in hospital but with a midwife, or on their own. A midwife charges more if the baby is a boy than if it's a girl. Even in the poorest places, where they charge five or 10 *colones*, they charge five for a girl and 10 for a boy. There are customs which make a woman, from the time of her birth, think of herself as a second-class person, created just to have children and do chores. I admire their endurance, the fact that despite having received nothing, they are capable of giving so much love to their children.

Pamela: Yet we know that the women in this country, as in other Latin American countries, are its strength.

Mercedes: Yes. In the Salvadorean 'process' the community has survived thanks to the women. In the repopulated communities it was they who risked going out to find medicines for the community. They did the cooking in the midst of bombardments. The problem is that we women have always lived for others, we have never used any energy for ourselves, to improve our own lives.

So I think feminism was born to say to women: 'You are wonderful human beings who have given so much. But you must also give a little to yourselves, make people respect you as you want your children to be respected.' Here in El Salvador the men themselves say that in the most difficult times during the war they got courage from the warmth of the women. According to them, not so much could happen to a woman — she wouldn't be recruited, and they [the security forces] didn't think she might be a political cadre. So the woman was the one who went out, who showed her face, who confronted the army sometimes, while the man stayed behind, full of fear. The men recognise that there were moments when only the women gave them courage. Now the women are back in their homes, but they played an important part in the survival of the community and their families.

Morena Herrera
Women for Dignity and Life

Morena Herrera is leader of the organisation Mujeres por la Dignidad y la Vida (Women for Dignity and Life), popularly known as the Dignas. Like nearly all the women's movements in El Salvador, the Dignas was founded on the initiative of one of the parties which make up the FMLN, in this case the National Resistance (RN).

How the Dignas began
Morena Herrera: At the beginning of 1990, the party in which I was a militant, the National Resistance, wanted to create an organisation to bring together women who worked in communal groupings, labour unions and above all the Committee of Mothers. Their aim was to contribute the women's point of view to the national political debate. They wanted a women's union, a reference point as they called it. They thought such an organisation could bring economic and material support to the party's revolutionary programme and to the war effort.

So those were the reasons behind the formation of Women for Dignity and Life, not our own belief as women that we should organise and enter on our own struggle.

Two of us had taken part in setting up a women's organisation in the Guazapa war zone in 1982, and this was a good experience, but it was exclusively in support of the war. Some of us commented at the time that this great effort did nothing to address any of our concerns. We supported military actions, helped care for the wounded, did many other things, but in terms of a specific struggle for women, at that time we did nothing.

But from the beginning of the Dignas we rebelled. We thought in terms of an organisation different from the one the National Resistance wanted. We didn't want to be just a support organisation where we didn't feel we were present as women, and which didn't address our needs. We didn't want a vertical organisation: many of us had experience of hierarchical structures. We wanted something that enabled us to function as women, as equals, despite having different histories and different situations.

So, right from the start there was a lot of tension with the party — over the question of the name, how we did things — there was constant disagreement. We even ended up without premises to meet in.

For our first national meeting the party directed us to organise a big public event, with the press, so as to make a political impact. We said no, we wanted to have a gathering of women. One woman found in a magazine the phrase 'Let's break the silence', and we adopted it and called the meeting 'Gathering of Women for Dignity and Life. Let's break the silence.' We didn't want the kind of meeting where only a few people spoke and the rest were passive, so we decided to talk about our own concerns as women and our proposed alternatives in the field of salaried work, the family, education, the media and the popular organisations. So we began on the road which later on we realised was the process of autonomy, although at the time we didn't know that was what we were doing! We call the first year of the Dignas 'the year of the NO'. There were a whole lot of 'NOs' but we didn't yet have a clear idea of what we positively wanted to do.

One of our many 'NOs' was to joining the Coordination of Women's Organisations (COM). You had to be linked to a party to join them and we knew that the history of coordinations of parties is that they have been very sectarian, and we wanted to find another kind of relationship among women.

'Unconscious feminists'

In our search we contacted some Mexican women's groups who began to send us materials and offered to do workshops with us. When they came in 1991 it was our first experience of feminist education. We had already seen some feminist materials and I had been to a feminist meeting in Argentina, but this was our first systematic experience. From then on we began an intensive educational process. Encountering feminist theories enabled us to give a name to processes we were already engaged in. I remember one of the women who came said to us: 'Where have you learnt all this about feminism?' We said: 'We don't know anything about feminism.' 'But these are feminist reflections you have been doing, didn't you know?' They were things we were already doing, but we didn't know what to call them.

The faith perspective

At the same time as the Dignas was developing, a parallel process was going on in the archbishopric. A group of us met there with a friend of mine, Gloria Guzmán, whom I had known since I was a child, to talk about women's issues from the faith perspective. We began to meet here in the neighbourhood of La Concepción, to reflect on how we felt as women in the church and to look at ourselves.

We didn't know then about the process of self-awareness of the feminist groups, but I realise that we were actually having consciousness-raising sessions, and that was useful for me later in sharing with the Dignas. I remember at one meeting a Colombian woman called Yolanda said: 'I have a question for you in this envelope.' We all went off to open our envelope, and when I opened mine, I saw a mirror and the question, 'Who am I?'. We began to talk about it in detail and we realised that in our first sessions we had always talked about the negative aspects of ourselves. But in those days of the Christian Women's Initiative, as we called it, we began to reflect on the positive aspects which we had not mentioned before, trying to rediscover them. These were very rich, personal experiences. We were not thinking so much of an organisation as of a space for reflection.

Moving towards independence

The year 1991 was one of great formative activity: coordinating the team, involving local groups, and beginning to set up projects with women in resettled communities in the war zones. In 1992 we identified some problems. We were not happy with the relationship between women in the countryside working in productive projects, and women in the town who did all the organising and provided the resources. Our idea was to train the women in the countryside to administer the projects themselves.

At the same time tensions between us and the party continued. Many of us had withdrawn from party activism, partly because our analysis of what was really happening in the country was different from theirs, and partly because they didn't accept us in the process of decision-making. At a deep personal level we felt hurt by what the *compañeros* — people who had been our comrades in the struggle — said about us, so we realised that we had not yet cut the umbilical cord. We knew that until we gave more importance to our own values, we would go on being just the feminine wing of the party.

Finally, in 1992 we spent a long day carrying out an analysis of our situation and at the end of it we made a transcendental decision: we would turn ourselves into an

---

Our integrity as women

After defining the terms of our political autonomy, many of us began leaving the party, one by one, without talking about it, without mutually agreeing it, simply by not attending party meetings. Perhaps because we had found in the Dignas a space we felt was our own, which answered our desire for personal and collective development, which allowed us to live political activism in a different way, without renouncing our integrity as women.

From 'Hacer Política Desde las Mujeres'
Mujeres por la Dignidad y la Vida, No 4, July 1993.

organisation for feminist political action. Together with other women's organisations we would become a force capable of making proposals and changing our lives. We saw that we were not taken into consideration in the peace accords. Despite the huge contribution women made to the war and to the process of struggle to have the accords implemented, women were simply not present. We put this forward very strongly and insisted that we were not being taken into account as women in the plans for national reconstruction either.

Pamela: How did things develop after that?

Morena: From that point on we decided on four lines of struggle which relate in different ways to the subordination we live in, like the majority of women. At different times one line of struggle will take priority over another but we intend them to be present in everything we do:

1. The struggle against violence. Domestic violence has certainly increased since the end of the war. In several communities in what used to be guerrilla-controlled zones we have seen that, when the combatants were demobilised, family violence increased. The return of the soldiers put pressure on the women to get back into the home and return to their traditional role in the family. We felt we had to deal with this as a national problem, because it affects most of the women in this country.

2. The quality of life for women. We want to evaluate this as a whole. It is not enough to look only at material conditions; one must also consider emotional conditions. Very little work is being done on the emotional healing and strengthening of women. The Truth Commission estimated that 73 per cent of the survivors are women, but there is no awareness of what this implies for the emotional reconstruction of society. We must concentrate on this, although we can't ignore the material conditions of life.

3. The democratisation of the country. We can contribute to this by promoting the participation of women, so that political programmes and agendas take on board women's issues and interests and more women are represented at decision-making levels.

4. Women's control over their bodies. Women need to have control over their own bodies, both in relation to sexuality and to their reproductive capacity, so that they can decide how many children they want to have and learn about their bodies.

We do all this in practice by organising in different sectors.

Repopulated communities
The largest sector, both in numbers and resources, is the repopulated communities. These are women who live in what were conflict zones, who have been carrying on a struggle at local level, organising against violence, dealing with specific cases, working to strengthen the leadership role of women, and trying to make sure that the contributions we make to solving the problems of the communities are visible and recognised.

The Christian sector
This group arose out of the Christian Women's Initiative (IMC). I was involved in it from when it began in 1990 until March 1991, when I had to stop taking an active part to look after my daughter. This group became well supported and coordinated and eventually became integrated with the Dignas. It gives us a component that some feminists don't understand, and query, but for us it is very important, because the Christian faith is a vital part of the identity of the women. In most cases it has been experienced as very oppressive, so we have made an effort to learn to reflect on gender themes from the Bible in a way that affirms our faith and transforms the situation of oppression. We have had good results, and good exchanges with women from other

churches. Out of these exchanges the Feminist Theological Circle developed; it has its own dynamic and brings an important subjective element to the Dignas.

One of the things that really impressed me about this group was the reading of the passage about the woman taken in adultery (*John* 8:1-11). It was powerful. The group pointed out how at the moment when the people were wanting to stone the woman, Jesus said: 'Do not sin, the sin of allowing yourself to be insulted, to have what you do decided for you.' This was a proposal for transformation that moved us greatly.

Although we have tried, we haven't yet succeeded in making this kind of contribution a permanent element in all the communities where the Dignas work. But we think that other Christian women in other zones, for example in the repopulated communities, must not be deprived of this type of reflection.

Pamela: There are Christians in the former war zones too.

Morena: Exactly. Most of the women in this country identify themselves as Christians, so theological reflection can contribute something to our organisation which it hasn't got, or isn't really taking advantage of.

For example, in our areas we have a programme for

Common sayings (especially in the countryside)

Nació un varón, envuélvalo en algodón.
Nació mujercita, quemar esta maldita.
A boy is born, wrap him in cotton wool.
A girl is born, burn the little wretch.

Cuando la comida es poca
a la niña no le toca.
When food is scarce
the girl doesn't get any.

---

training midwives, older women. On the technical level we try to enable them to give better care, to accompany the women during their pregnancy and after the birth. But we are also trying to get them to act more in favour of women. For example, here the midwives charge more if a boy is born than a girl, so we are working with the midwives on this. Also, recently we had the case of a woman who was dying from inflammation of the veins, and she would not have an abortion because she was going to have all the children God wanted her to have — she and her husband were both very Christian people. The work of the Christian women was to say to the woman that God loves her too, that she should see God not only as a Father ruling over her, but also as a Mother who understands her. In the end the woman decided to have an abortion and the husband supported the decision. So we have to try to combine our efforts, bringing together work to improve the physical conditions and work relating to awareness and emotions.

Emotional aspects of motherhood

Pamela: Morena, I am interested in this report *Social and Emotional Aspects of Motherhood* which the Dignas published, could you say something about this?

Morena: Last year [1993] we ran a workshop on the emotional consequences of motherhood in time of war. Forty-four women came, not only from the Dignas, and we talked about what it had meant to be a mother during the war years. It was something that brought out a great deal of pain. That showed us that we had to work on the emotional side, so we got the support of the Jesuits for a pilot programme. We looked for psychologists who could work on feminine emotions from a feminist perspective, and we didn't find any here. So we invited a Spanish woman to come here for two months, on two occasions, and we had groups working on mental health, we organised interviews and began to look at the emotional side of women. At the same time we ran a course for 15 psychiatrists — two of them are working with the Dignas now — in order to continue the mental health programme.

Political participation
We ran a programme of training in citizenship, which is still going on and which is geared more to the elections at the moment, so that women know how the electoral mechanisms work, how to get effectively involved and the importance of getting their documents.

Mujeres '94
Now of course we are working on a women's political platform, which we call Women '94. One of our demands is for the National Civil Police to include a specialised service for women victims of sexual violence and domestic ill-treatment, an issue which we worked on here. Then we did an investigation into the reasons for the discrimination against women in the peace accords and the transfer of lands.[46] There the mechanisms are subtle. If a woman has a husband, her husband appears as the tenant of the land and has access to the credit. She doesn't appear. But what happens in these communities is that a man has two or three women, each one with her children, but only the man is taken into account. That kind of thing. It's a struggle with the FMLN Land Commission and the government Land Commission. But the [land transfer] programme has stalled, only 25 per cent has been implemented.

Last year we investigated the political participation of women, identifying the percentage of female participation in all the parties and in state jobs, and developing Women '94's proposal about quotas of participation at decision-making level. Those are the sort of things we do. We have two small support groups: one for projects, which works in this little room, and a small administration unit.

Pamela: Have the different women's organisations worked together on all this?

---

46. Transfer of land to landless people and ex-combatants following the war.

Morena: Yes, we formed the platform of Women '94 together. The platform is an effort in which nearly all the women's organisations take part. Unfortunately, we are not yet all united on how to carry forward the struggle for our demands. This is partly because the parties, including the FMLN, still do not grasp the significance of women in this country. We continue to be seen as mothers. There is still no perception of our importance as women. I am convinced that it is a process of building up our strength.

Women and the preferential option for the poor

Pamela: What about the church's preferential option for the poor? Where do the women come in?

Morena: The preferential option for the poor was not translated into an option for the poorest of the poor — the women. In our group we felt that if we did not succeed in incorporating this, there would be a gap that it would be important to fill. We were able to make a contribution at the CELAM [Latin American Bishops' Conference] meeting in Santo Domingo in 1992. The auxiliary bishop of San Salvador [Monseñor Gregorio Rosa Chávez] was coordinating preparatory meetings and he called us to take part. We presented papers. In the final document [*Women in the Church and Latin American Culture*], in the part on women in the church, there are some things we didn't say and others that we did. There was a lot of interesting discussion around that document.

Pamela: So you think that document doesn't contain everything you said?

Morena: Not everything that we put forward, no. There were some rather daring proposals. For example, one woman said: 'The church has to make its confession before the people of God, for the sin of patriarchy.'

Ana Gloria and Mónica

Ana Gloria is the main support, both financial and moral, of
her extended family in San Salvador, and a 'tough lady'.

Ana Gloria: I am 40 and at the moment I make my living as
a saleswoman for industrial chemical products. The good
Lord thinks so much of me that he gives me enough to eat
and no more. I thank God for this, because if I had more I
might forget those who are in need. And we really do need
God's help — thanks to him I have been able to keep my
family going. Not only my immediate family of daughter
and husband — because my husband doesn't live with us,
although he does help our daughter — but I cover the
expense of this house and my father, with just some help
from my older sister. So we manage to keep going.

We are a big family, and we all live in the same house:
Papá, my sister, her husband and two small children, my
daughter Mónica and myself: seven people living in the
same house. My father bought this house when houses
were cheaper. It was a sacrifice for him to bring us all from
where we were living, but thank God we have a house. But
we still have to pay for the water, light, telephone.

I would say we are a family of the lower middle class.
Before the war we classified people into lower, lower
middle, middle middle, upper middle and upper. I
consider we would have been middle middle.

Marigold: When you were young, what did you expect of
life?

Ana: We were brought up with my mother, because I can't
remember that my father was ever with us at that time. He
didn't have a say in our education.

When we were children, we two sisters lived with my mother. We couldn't even buy a toy and there wasn't such a variety as there is now. We played with stones, bricks, nails. We used to put a skirt on some of the nails so that they could be the women and the others were men. We played at markets. We didn't have a television in those days, so I used to go to the neighbours to watch TV. All the children used to meet there: we sat on the steps and fought for the place where you could see through a crack in the door. We didn't have skates or dolls or a bicycle.

I think a child's character is formed when she is small. Because of our childhood with all its limitations, we have been able to survive because we have strong characters.

Marigold: So you didn't feel that your role in life was to become a housewife?

Ana: No. We had our tasks, like washing and ironing our clothes. My mother washed and ironed other people's clothes to keep us, and she also had the money my father gave her.

Marigold: Did you study?

Ana: Yes. My father paid school expenses, pens and pencils, uniform and so on. My mother looked after our moral education.

Marigold: And this was before the war?

Ana: Yes, long before. I am 40 now. The conflict lasted 12 years, I was 28 when the war began.

Marigold: And you were working in your 20s and 30s?

Ana: Yes, I began to work when I graduated as a bilingual secretary, which is not an academic career. So I have been working since I was 18.

Marigold: Did you feel then that you had the same opportunities as the men?

Ana: Yes, that depends on each person's aspirations — it's a struggle. I was able to work and get funding to begin a university career, but unfortunately I found it heavy going. Later I married and the university was left behind.

Marigold: How do you now see your role as a woman? You have several roles: you work, you bring up your daughter, you are responsible for keeping the family going. How do you do all this? Where do you get the strength for it?

Ana: I owe it to the education my mother gave me. She had a very strong character. I think that if she had not brought us up like that, we would have been people of weak character and we wouldn't have been able to bear our burdens. Thank God we Salvadoreans are workers and don't give in easily. Here's an anecdote: in the 1980s the travelling saleswomen used to say after a massacre: 'Get the dead out of the way, I want to put down my basket of tomatoes (or whatever it might be).' That shows you how hardworking we are. We carry on our shoulders the responsibility for getting food to our families. Nature itself gives this strength. I know that my country has suffered a lot, and that if we are still alive and have hope for the future, it's because of that same perseverance in doing the best for the family.

Marigold: Have you any opportunities for being with other women, to talk and support each other?

Ana: Yes, there is a very solid community where I work, and we earn quite a lot. Most people earn between 5,000 and 10,000 *colones*. I earn 5,000 and that's a good salary, given that there are academic professionals who earn less. But there is an unusual situation in my business: most of the employees are self-sufficient women. There are three men among 30 women. We women think that for a man to approach us with romance in mind, he would have to earn double what we earn, so as to meet our needs. In other words, he couldn't. Most of the women are divorced with children. We are so tough, we women, that we practically have no need of men.

Mónica, Ana's daughter, is an intelligent and sensitive 13-year-old whose life in the capital is more restricted than Silvia's (see page 184). Apart from a few family outings, she only goes to school. Much of the information that comes into the house is ARENA propaganda. When we talked with her, she was 13 and studying at the College of the Divine Providence.

Marigold: You were born in 1980, so you have spent nearly all your life in a time of war. What has that meant to you?

Mónica: It has been very difficult for me and for all children, because when we wanted to go for a family outing or a walk, we could never do it without worrying. We knew we were exposing ourselves to danger, because they used to capture families and kill them. Children know what is happening, and every time we went out, we heard shots.

Marigold: Both sides said that what they wanted was the good of the people — if that was so, why were they fighting?

Mónica: I think they were fighting because of envy. There was no need for them to fight and I think that, instead of fighting and killing so many innocent people, they should have thought about what they were doing before they started that war.

Marigold: Do you think there was a way for the poor people in the country and the cities to get out of their extreme poverty without this war?

Mónica: Yes. If there hadn't been the war they would have been much better off, because they were the ones who suffered. In the city there was not much war. It was in the country where the fighting was, and the guerrillas harmed the poor people and communities. Sometimes they stole their things and took over their houses to defend themselves, so things were more critical for them than for us here in the city.

Marigold: What were the soldiers doing in the countryside?

Mónica: They were marauding all over the place and people were very frightened of both sides. For the poor people it was the same, they were always in the same danger.

Marigold: Do you think that now with the peace accords life will be better for everyone?

Mónica: Yes. The people in the country will be able to go back to their activities, have their bit of land and cultivate it. It will be better for us here, too, because we will not be so scared any more.

Marigold: In your school are there boys and girls?

Mónica: Yes, not many boys, but there are some.

Marigold: And do the girls feel the same as the boys, just as intelligent? Do they treat you the same?

Mónica: Yes, both groups are the same because we are all people, like everyone else. We have our rights and there is no reason for the boys to feel superior to us.

Marigold: And, at home, are boys beginning to help in the house?

Mónica: Yes, they have to help, because if they don't, the

girls start shouting: 'Mamá, why do you make me help and not him?' Both must help just the same.

Marigold: And do you feel that you have the same opportunities to study and to work as the boys do?

Mónica: Yes, I think so, because both boys and girls, men and women, have to make their way as best way they can. It is the same for all of us.

Marigold: What are your own hopes for the future?

Mónica: I mean to study and have a career and then get married.

Marigold: What do you think is a good age to get married?

Mónica: Twenty-seven, so that I can start a career first.

Marigold: And would you go on working after getting married?

Mónica: Yes, I would work to support my family and my husband would work too.

Marigold: Would you expect him to help you in the house?

Mónica: Yes, I would — we would help each other.

Drugs culture
Marigold: Mónica, could you tell me something about the *maras* [street gangs] that people have been talking about?

Mónica: They are small groups of people who get together to do harm. They have no good aim, they only think of creating disorder; their life consists of creating havoc, taking drugs, and that sort of thing.
    When I was driving along an avenue one day, the *maras*

came from the centre of the city, creating a disturbance. They took a bus, took all the people out, they parked the bus across the street so that nobody had access to the streets or the public services, they hurt many people and broke windows.

They have a war with gangs from other schools and colleges. Everyone is afraid of them. That day, I was in the car with my mother and we tried to avoid them, but they came along on the other side of the street, breaking the windows of the microbuses and of the urban service. Then they came up behind us, wanting to break our windows, but they didn't manage it.

They put fear into everyone and I don't think that's right. The social services here can't do anything; there are too many of them, they are like ants. Salvadorean youth is becoming degenerate. With the drugs, they get worse. A friend of mine from the institute where I study was blinded by a stone thrown in her eye. If there are authorities who can come and do something, we ask for help, please, because it is dangerous.

Marigold: How is it that these youths have nothing good to do?

Mónica: I think they are a bit mad. Our country is something of a copy-cat, and the *maras* come originally from the United States. Salvadoreans want to copy them, and they act exactly the same as they do there, painting graffiti and so on. I don't know how they can do so much pointless damage. Their only aim is to fight and do damage and I can't explain why they do it.

Marigold: Who gives them the drugs?

Mónica: Drugs come especially from the nearest countries, Nicaragua, Panama, especially Colombia, and the young people look for ways to get money so that they can buy.

Marigold: Are there programmes which try to help these young drug addicts?

Mónica: Yes, there is the Foundation FUNDASALVA, which is trying to help in every way to put young people on the right path. There is a new campaign which says: 'I can live without drugs.' We young people have marched to protest against drugs, but the people who are doing the harm go on doing it. But no progress will be made without the help of young people who are alright; we ourselves have to work on this.

The *maras* are gangs of youths who roam the streets and create violent disturbances. Towards the end of 1995 the violence escalated to murder, probably as a result of gang rivalry and territorial disputes. One cause of this is the exclusion of young people from educational and work opportunities.

This exclusion would explain in large part why the young have been at the centre of the main socio-political protest movements in the country since the 1950s. But whereas in the 1960s and 1970s their demands found expression in political and revolutionary organisations, in the 1990s they have turned to street gangs. Another fundamental difference is that the groups in the 1960s and 1970s believed in the possibility of political change, while the young people of the 1990s do not. Unless attention is paid to the desire for cultural identity and a space in which to live it, solutions proposed for the problem will be doomed to failure.

The grave economic situation of many urban families is another important factor. A Salvadorean social worker reported that the Ministry of Education is very worried about the *maras*, and has tried to combat the problem by lengthening school hours until 3 pm. The main result appears to have been that many young people either faint from hunger during afternoon classes or go off to rob in order to buy food.

Silvia

Silvia is 12, much the same age as Mónica (see previous chapter). She has known greater dangers and hardships but has also had a wider experience in many ways.

Paul Godden, a Quaker Peace and Service worker in the returned refugee community of Nueva Esperanza, had this conversation in January 1995, shortly before Silvia's 13th birthday. Silvia is an adopted daughter (in fact, niece) of Andrea (see page 85). She is named after the murdered nun, Sister Silvia Arriola, of the Little Community (see page 55).

Paul Godden: I want to ask you about your family. Where did you live before you lived here?

Silvia: In San Salvador. I was born there, and at one and a half months they took me off the breast. As my parents and all my brothers were in the war, my mother left me with Mami Andrea and went off to work. [Silvia's mother's job was to go into town to buy supplies and smuggle them out to the guerrillas, an immensely dangerous task.] When my parents learned that Mami was in a refuge, they started to bring her my brothers and sisters — the littlest ones — and as they got big enough they took them away to the front and one of them died there. From our family, 15 boys were killed very young, including one of my brothers at the age of 14. They had taken him to the front when he was eight, where he acted as a messenger for the FPL [People's Liberation Army] and the ERP [People's Revolutionary Army]. When he was 10 they sent him over this way to San Vicente — to the most dangerous zones — and that is where he died.

After we left the refuge my Mami worked for a while in the capital, but she did not feel safe there because it was obvious that we came from the countryside. So, in order for me to be nearer my family, she took me to Zamorán. Then from Zamorán we applied to come and live here in Nueva Esperanza.

Paul: What was it like in Zamorán in the war years?

Silvia: Tough. Sometimes the soldiers came and took people out of their houses and afterwards they never came back.

Paul: Did the soldiers come through Zamorán every day?

Silvia: Yes, every day.

Paul: But at the same time did you have contact with the *compas* in their camps?

Silvia: Yes. My Mami used to sew things for the *compas* and that was dangerous because if she was caught doing that she'd have been in for it. My Mami and an aunt of mine were the ones there who had a sewing machine, and they were the ones who took charge of making them trousers and shirts — at night they started sewing. If they were sewing during the day somebody would keep watch to give them warning that the soldiers were coming. Then they would bury all their things.

Once the *compas* were in our house eating when the warning came that the soldiers were coming through the coconut grove near our house, so they slipped out another way and left the food. When the soldiers came they were very suspicious and it was a close call that they didn't accuse my Mami.

Paul: They were suspicious because there was half-eaten food?

Silvia: What my Mami did was to throw it to the animals, but since there are always traces of footsteps in the dust I grabbed the broom. 'What are you doing?' they asked. 'Sweeping,' I said. 'Didn't the guerrillas come this way?' they asked. 'What guerrillas?' I said. I pretended to be stupid and then the neighbours came to see what was going on so they didn't do anything to us. When the *compas* passed through it was our job to sweep away the tracks in the dust — once they got into the woods there was no more danger. But where we were it was very dangerous.

Paul: Weren't you afraid?

Silvia: Of course — except that they had a radio transmitter and they gave us one [a receiver] so that they could give us warning.

Paul: Was the community of Zamorán very organised at that time?

Silvia: No, it was very disorganised. There were families linked to the military who acted as 'fingers' and that was the fear. There were people there who told the army captain that my Mami was sewing uniforms; he came into the house and abused Mami. So the family told Mami she had better get out. So Mami went.

Paul: Did you go to school in Zamorán?

Silvia: No, there was no school. My sister-in-law used to teach first and second grade, but then she married my brother and the captain told her she mustn't give classes any more. They were hunting my brother to kill him.

Paul: What do you hope to do in the future? Will you go on studying?

Silvia: Yes, as far as I can get.

Paul: Do you want to do something special?

Silvia: I'd like to be a teacher most — but I don't know.

Paul: Do you go to the pastoral group?

Silvia: Yes, I'm in the adolescents' group. At the moment we're discussing the kind of problems that girls have to face — for instance not getting pregnant too young. Waiting until you've made a proper commitment to someone and finished your studies — then you can think about it.

Paul: And what is your understanding about the conflict?

Silvia: Well, they say it started because of the church. My Mami went through the war with Honduras and then came and had to go through the war here.

Paul: So what happened in the church?

Silvia: In 1979 Mami couldn't go on being a catechist — which is what she was. She couldn't go on working with Monseñor Romero and then he was killed.

Paul: So what hopes have you got for the future now that the situation has changed quite a bit?

Silvia: That things will go on changing, because the war has stopped. But there is still a war in society — a lot of robbery and delinquency — things haven't changed all that much.

Ana Guadalupe Martínez
From student to FMLN militant to vice-president of the Legislative Assembly

In August of 1992 Ana Guadalupe Martínez of the People's Revolutionary Army, a faction of the FMLN, spoke in an interview with CIIR of her involvement with the FMLN and the armed struggle and of how it began.

Ana Guadalupe Martínez: I was in the last year of my degree work — it was 1968 — and there was a teachers' strike. I didn't know what it was all about, but I was in a [state] school where there were opportunities to mix with young people from the popular sectors to hear about their concerns. So we began to understand why the teachers were striking and to support them.

Q: What were the major influences on you at that time?

Ana: There were two. One was my mother, who had a profound sense of Christian solidarity with the people. The other was that of Simón Bolívar — we had books on him in our house and I read about the independence, the epic crossing of the Andes, of all the difficulties. That mixture of Christian influence and Bolívar was decisive in my joining the people's struggle in El Salvador. Being a Catholic was important to me, and when I was able to understand what solidarity was, and what a Christian should be for others, I thought: 'Well, why not fight for the people who need it?'

Q: What was your first political action?

Ana: I don't know which was the first conscious political stance. In the teachers' strike it was a feeling of solidarity with people who were struggling, then in the university I began to take part in activities of the student movement, but more from a feeling of rebelliousness than from a clear understanding of what the students' struggle was all about. The whole question of political participation was a later development in my case.

Q: How long were you politically active before you had to leave the country?

Ana: They recruited me for the armed struggle in 1973, and I was captured in 1976, when I was with the guerrillas. Once I was freed, my security problem was very serious and it was very difficult to work in San Salvador. The war fronts were barely beginning, so my work after liberation was done from abroad, although I came back for long periods.

Q: Was it a difficult decision to join the armed struggle or did it seem a natural, logical way of responding to reality?

Ana: Well, the way I became committed was rather special. They didn't ask me directly: 'Do you want to be a guerrilla?' It began when I was asked if I could help by hiding in my house a person who had problems with the National Guard in a district of San Salvador. I still lived in Santa Ana at that time. I said yes. They told me the person might arrive that afternoon to stay until better arrangements for his security could be made. I waited all afternoon, wondering if he was coming or not. Night came, and he didn't arrive. The next day I was very anxious, and in the afternoon they came to tell me they had solved the problem and he was going to stay in San Salvador. It turned out that the person was Joaquín Villalobos.[47] I think my willingness to say yes was important to them, and from then on they began to ask me to do other small tasks, like going to find things, helping to transport material (they never told me what kind of material). That was how I began to participate

---

47. Villalobos became leader of the ERP, one of the five 'fronts' of the FMLN. See note 34, page 96.

and it was then I began to realise there were guerrilla groups in El Salvador.

Joining was easy because they did not confront me with the question of whether or not I wanted to be part of an armed struggle. The problem arose much later on when they asked me to take part in an armed action. This was a very difficult moment for me, when I had to make an irreversible commitment, and it wasn't a decision taken quickly. But I had no doubt that what I was doing was right, and that helped me over that moment.

Q: Were there many other women making these decisions, or were you exceptional?

Ana: There were several of us students, because the phenomenon of women's participation at this time was linked to the fact that the student movement was extremely active, and this made it possible for women to join as equals with men.

Q: Did you raise and discuss women's issues within the movement, or were you not interested in that side of the struggle?

Ana: Certainly there was discussion, not of women as a group, but of the woman as a militant. The question was: 'Are you going to take part unconditionally and make the revolution your life? Then you can't have children yet.' A couple's decision not to have children was perhaps the basic element that made it possible for the woman to aspire to take part with equal opportunities with the men. That discussion didn't come from the women, it came from the men, and it made a great impression on us. It made us take decisions of that kind and I think it allowed us to reach leadership levels, because we had nothing to do other than work for the revolution for 10 or 15 years of our productive life. It was like a vow, we had to make a vow — it was a total commitment of the person. This was something we had to take on and we accepted it.

I began to think of children when I was 30. My pregnancy was my own decision, but it caused a huge stir at the heart of the organisation. This was in 1983, when things were not yet very clear and the prospects were of a very long struggle, but I said: 'Well, new generations are coming on and they will replace us. We have a right to the woman's part.' But at the beginning there was much discussion, and it made a big impression on me when they said: 'Here, the fundamental thing is the revolution. We hope you understand that children take up time. You won't be able to look after a child, you will have a conflict between the attention given to the children and your revolutionary task, so it is better to decide not to have children.' The proposition was as crude as that. I think it was a correct position because it made us participate unconditionally in the service of what we believed in, which was the revolution.

After the peace accords

In January 1994 Ana Guadalupe Martínez was an FMLN representative in the Legislative Assembly of El Salvador, and vice-president of that assembly. When we met her she was fully engaged in the FMLN's electoral campaign but she took time to give us her views on the change in the role of women brought about by the end of the fighting.

Pamela: Ana, during the war women proved themselves capable of carrying out a wide range of tasks, but some women have told us that now the war is over they have had to go back to their domestic role. Would you say that is so, from your experience?

Ana: I think that's true. I share that feeling. The war was exceptional, so women were able to leave their kids with relatives and go off to do any sort of work. This happened to me. I knew someone was looking after my children and I never worried about whether they were eating or

191

studying or not. Now that the war is over, it is my responsibility — and you can't imagine how difficult it is.

I'll give you an example. I have a woman who helps me with the children, but once a month she goes home for four days. As she is the only woman I have to help me, and my husband also works in the political field, when this woman is away for four days, I have no one to look after the children. So each time I have to think where I can leave them. Today, for instance, they've been alone all day, and they are 10, nine and six years old. We lock them up in the house. If I stay with them all morning, I don't work. I have a better chance of solving the problem than many women because I have a house, a key, a refrigerator, so they can eat. The eldest has to look after the younger ones. I have a phone — they've just rung to tell me to take a cooked chicken home because there was nothing for lunch. That's a concrete example of the many problems that have arisen for me in fulfilling my role of political leader.

I'll give you another example. Yesterday I had to be in a meeting. The woman who looks after my children was not there, so I was going to take them with me to the meeting. I like them to begin to be politically aware and take part, and they like it. But my husband was going to stay with the six-year-old. At 7am, when I was due to leave for the meeting, he had a severe pain, a kidney problem. So I couldn't go to the meeting, I had to give him an injection — after years of not having done such a thing — it was Sunday so there was no one else. In the end I gave him three injections that day. But I couldn't go to the meeting and I didn't know what to do. Do you know what I did? I sent the girls in the car, with a note for the eldest girl to read at the meeting, so that people could understand that it was not disrespect — because people sometimes think that in today's new situation you don't want to spend time with them. So the two girls went off — they were overcome, because there were 2,000 people there, and they had to read my message.

These are the kinds of difficulties I have, and I have

more options than, say, the wife of an ex-combatant who has no resources at all, and in addition is a single mother. She has to try and resolve her family's problems, her children's, her own, and also do her share politically. These women end up in the house again, doing what they did before the war.

Pamela: How do the men see the women now? Do they see them differently after the war experience when women did so much, or do they still consider that their place is in the home?

Ana: There are two complementary factors. First, education and, second, the debate over the kind of role women should fulfil in these new conditions, above all on the left. I have an established position, but, especially if the problems I was talking about are not resolved, they are less likely to be able to take part. And if a man has enough time, because he hasn't got our problems — children, the home — then clearly the one who is going to be able to develop in a responsible job is the man. So I think there is a twofold situation: the mentality [of the men], and material conditions. If material conditions are not favourable, then however capable a woman may be, she will never develop. The same is true if the mentality is such that she is not allowed to participate.

Doing the theology of memory: Counting crosses and resurrections

by **Marcella Althaus-Reid**

Dr Marcella Althaus-Reid is a lecturer in Christian Ethics and Practical Theology at New College, University of Edinburgh. Born in Argentina, she first studied theology at ISEDET (Union Theological Seminary), Buenos Aires, one of the leading centres for liberation theology in Latin America. Marcella has worked among deprived communities in both Argentina and Scotland and written on feminist hermeneutics, popular education and liberation theology. She is a Quaker.

Resurrection as a community issue

How do people resurrect? In a future moment outside history and with trumpets and angels coming from heaven? Or in the tension of the present, but 'not yet among us', reign of God?

Latin American art and poetry are full of images of resurrection. The popular painters from Nicaragua depict the resurrection of the body with the familiar faces of people killed during the revolution leaving their graves. They are wearing jeans and shirts, smiling at each other, and giving us the impression of a community resurrecting from death. The fact is that Jesus's resurrection was also a community event: women and men witnessed how he came back from death, walked among them and continued the dialogue which existed before his crucifixion. Every death changes the life of the survivors because some humanity is removed from them. So it is legitimate to think that, starting with Jesus's resurrection, a whole community of people who suffered his loss when he was crucified came back to life again. Their eyes were opened in the sense that death took on another meaning; the resurrection became the paradigm showing us the durability and indestructibility of life and justice.

Nobody resurrects alone

We were reading the Bible, praying and reading the newspaper at the same time, in the disorderly fashion so typical of small community groups in Latin America. Someone had brought a brief editorial article written by Gustavo Gutiérrez called 'News of The Cross and Resurrection', in which the Peruvian theologian reflected on the death of the martyrs of El Salvador: Segundo Montes, Amando López, Joaquín López y López, Ignacio Martín-Baró, Ignacio Ellacuría, Juan Ramón Moreno, Julia Elba Ramos and Celina Ramos.

> From El Salvador we have received news of the Cross [...] from a country with such a meaningful name ('The Saviour'). The Jesuits and the two women were threatened and killed because of their testimony to justice. From El Salvador we also received news of resurrection, materialised by the strength of the Holy Spirit. The good news of the resurrection.[48]

After this reading an old woman said that perhaps we do not die alone, because we are all part of a community; whenever someone dies in the community, the community also dies a little. In fact, El Salvador died every day with every brother and sister murdered. Things cannot be the same again after a death in the community, but as the death is shared, so, the hope is, will be the resurrection.

The contribution of the theology of memory

The women of El Salvador exemplify what it means for Christian people to be the witnesses of the cross and the resurrection, and this is one of the most important

---

48. G Gutiérrez, 'Noticias de Cruz y Resurrección', in *Páginas*, December 1989.

contributions to the action and reflection process of liberation theology in Latin America. This is a Theology of Memory, counting crosses and resurrections, and it is being developed by poor women in Latin America. Theirs is an obstinate exercise in the belief in life amid death squads and the politics of hunger and dehumanisation, which produces infinite forms of little everyday deaths in the life of the poor. Dead dreams and plans for a better future are resurrected by a community of women remembering. They are part of a wider community of Latin American women who are still claiming the bodies of their dead, such as the Madres de Plaza de Mayo in Argentina and the widows of Guatemala. Even their white head scarves have come to characterise 'the ones who remember'. But remembrance is also memorial and celebration, all of them are closely associated in the Scriptures as belonging to the communitarian creed of the people of God.

Towards a collective women's theology of memory

The stories shared by the Salvadorean women are about the essentially collective act of doing theology by women survivors of the years of war and pain in El Salvador. It has elements of remembrance, but as part of a reflection which is projected on to the future, to the utopia of the kingdom that is created from everyday life, with its tragedy but also its simplicity. By calling it a 'collective women's theology' we engage in reclaiming the theological validity of the praxis of the poor,[49] in this case poor women of El Salvador. Basically the Theology of Memory is a methodology, a walk which starts with the silenced history of the poor women in Latin America, finds in them 'that of God' present (what we can call resurrections, that is the presence of God in the memories of life and death) and continues the path begun by liberation theology. The sources of reflection are life itself from the perspective of women living under political, socio-economic, domestic and military violence. The

---

49. Praxis as used in liberation theology is the continuous process of action-reflection-action. As practised by poor people, this is not considered by some to be theologically valid.

reading of the Bible is done 'outside the Bible', through the search for motives, motivating life-events, and what have been called 'events of liberation' which coincide with other events of liberation in the Scriptures such as exodus or the resurrection, for example. This women's popular theology is basically hermeneutical; that is, it interprets the word and the world simultaneously. At the same time it is like a dialogue because it is done in a participative way in community, and has elements of openness to new understandings which has become part of processes of social and spiritual transformation.

A theology of memory becomes a theology of blossoming

A poor person blossoms when they feel they count for something.

Ernestina Rivera[50]

There are two kinds of 'popular theology'. Both are pertinent to the life and needs of the poor, but the theological subject differs. There is a popular theology developed with the poor by professional theologians, rescuing key issues from their lives as a basis for a theological reflection related to their everyday experience of deprivation and suffering. This type of theology requires a serious commitment on the theologian's part to what Leonardo Boff has called 'a call to evangelical poverty', that is, becoming poor as part of a theological option. The results of such theological processes are usually politically mobilising and transformative; the elements of denunciation of injustices and the annunciation of the Good News are an important part of the ongoing conscientisation which this theology carries with it. Sisters Peggy O'Neill and Jean Ryan give an example of that kind of conscientisation work done with the people.

The other type of 'popular theology' is also transformative and *conscientizadora*, but it is not developed by professional theologians choosing poverty as an

---

50. From López Vigil, 1993, *op cit.*

evangelical option. Instead, it is worked out by the poor themselves. Such a theology usually presents a challenge not only to structures of oppression, but to Christianity itself owing to its critical stance arising from the historical experiences of the poor in Latin America. In other words, this is a critical Theology of Memory done from the underside of history. This is the theology which 'makes people blossom', because it restores the principle of the authority of the believers, and respects their right to express their particular experience of God in their lives, according to their cultures, traditions and political circumstances. This 'theology of blossoming' is the one lived by women in El Salvador.

'Blossoming' is the metaphor for a women's theology characterised by changes, growth, transformation, and especially, for a corporeal theology born out of women's bodies and their suffering during the war. Memories blossom and produce new actions and reflections, going from the crosses women have counted on mass graves to the annunciation of the community resurrection. The characteristics of the 'theology of blossoming' coming from the reflections of the women in these pages are:

1. the distinctiveness of the theological subject of reflection, which is women, and communities seen through women's eyes. The theological focus they use for their reflections, and the theological method where 'memory' is a key category.

2. the 'action-reflection-action' circle, and the efficacy of this theological process. For instance, the consequences of their reflections in terms of a new ecclesiology, that is, a new way of being church.

1. Women of El Salvador: their theological focus

What, then, are the theological resources used in the circle of action and reflection illustrated by the women who have shared their stories in this book? Some distinctive elements are how they use the Bible and the new way of interpreting old traditions of the church. However, it would be interesting to consider whether the Bible has been used by all the women or by an educated minority under special circumstances — for instance, under the leadership of priests or religious sisters.

The testimonies on the use of the Bible

Sister Mark spoke about the situation in Gotera, Morazán, during the days of the war and the lack of opportunities in formal education. For instance, a woman called María confessed that she did not know how to read or write, and joined the bible study group only to hear the readings and to write the word of God 'in her heart.' Another woman, Lucía B, comments that she cannot say much about the Bible because she is not 'well educated'. In Latin America, for poor communities who are illiterate in Spanish, the reading of the Bible is perceived as exclusive to the educated priesthood, and carries with it the authority and prestige of the well-off people with education. When Mercedes Cañas talks about the miserable conditions of life of women in some regions of El Salvador where they 'sit on a stone, with another stone in their hand, crushing olive stones one by one', because after the war their poverty is even more extreme, she is indirectly questioning Christianity as well as raising issues of extreme deprivation. Therefore, it is legitimate to ask what is the place of the Bible as a theological resource for these women.

The question to ask is how representative the reading of the Bible could be among illiterate communities struggling to survive because, as Cañas says, 'from salt upwards everything is a problem'. How can the woman in Nuevo Gualcho find time or energy for bible studies after her long day of washing in the river and grinding corn to make *tortillas* for her family? Yet it seems that the Bible has a place, although different groups use it in different ways. Educated or not, the key point is that they all start to 'read' the Bible first of all 'outside the Bible', that is, from their *realidad*. Their lives become a living text where God manifests Godself, and from there, the events of liberation in the Scripture are rescued and reflected upon in a circle of '*realidad*-Bible-*realidad*.'

Reading the Bible 'outside the Bible'

The base community of San Antonio Abad is an example of women doing theology through bible study groups, which also includes the reading of texts such as selected documents from the Roman Catholic church. Sister Mark and Sister Jean followed Carlos Mesters's approaches for their study programmes, that is, a dialogue which includes people's experiences interwoven with the experiences of the poor in the biblical texts.[51]

The *rezadoras* ('prayer ladies') such as Rosy use the Bible in their rosary prayer meetings in a radical way. Rosy has developed a popular liturgy which includes praying with the Scriptures, understanding how to relate the texts to the *realidad* and using her guitar and music as vehicles to communicate with people beyond words.

Their *realidad* was the *realidad* of the war: fleeing from the massacres through the mountains, and experiencing all sorts of suffering related to their attempt to escape their pursuers, leaving behind their homes and villages. This was called *la guinda*, and became a theological focus for a reflection on death and resurrection.

The *guinda*

The *guinda* seems to be a real life example of the biblical paradigm of exodus. Lucía O, sharing her experience of the *guinda* from Cuscatlán to Santa Ana, never mentions the Exodus, although the story reminds us of the flight of the Hebrews pursued by the Egyptian troops. A professional theologian could have related the events described in Exodus to the flight from Cuscatlán: the pharaoh's soldiers would be represented by 12,000 soldiers sent to kill the people from Cuscatlán in the 'Guazapa 10' Operation; the leadership of Moses by the *muchachos* who asked the community to leave; the presence of the pillar of cloud and fire, would become the constant words of the *muchachos*: 'Keep going, keep going.' However, the community which

---

51. See Carlos Mesters's *Defenseless Flower* (1989), where he recounts the methods used in Brazil to read the Scriptures with the people.

escaped through the mountains reflected theologically not on exodus but on death and resurrection. They took the story of *Luke* 8:42, because the community experienced death, and yet they were spared. The theology of blossoming seems to find in 'life' a permanent focus of theological reflection and renewal. The old memories of liberation in the Bible find new meaning among the poor. The women from El Salvador understood their experience of the *guinda* in the light of the miracles of the *New Testament*, passing from death to life, in a paradigm of community resurrection.

The living tradition of the church

The text of the Bible is read not only in relation to life, but in a permanent elaboration of the traditions of the Roman Catholic church. These women stress the living tradition of the church, by the way they reflect on their faith in relation to the war. For instance, the prayer to the saints for protection, characteristic of the popular religiosity of the poor in Latin America, becomes a prayer and reflection on the lives of the contemporary saints who have laid down their lives working for the reign of God, through the pursuit of justice and peace.

Bernarda gives testimony of how she prayed to the 'blessed blood of Monseñor Romero' for deliverance from the massacre of Amatitán. As part of the process of reading the Bible 'outside the Bible', the blood of a just man appeals to God for justice. In this case, the Abel of *Genesis* 4:10 is Monseñor Romero whose blood cries out to God for the crimes against the people of El Salvador. This blood from Romero protecting Bernarda and her child is then a visible sign of justice, and at the same time, a sign of the resurrection of the martyred saints among the people.

Another example is the story of the alcoholic dancing at the grave side of the woman 'who never failed to give him a *tortilla*'. Here solidarity has also become a sign of living faith in Christ. The tradition of the church concerning miracles becomes tangible in the life of the community through the testimonies of solidarity and hope. The historical testimonies of miracles in the life of the church are not remembered because for these communities 'God is a God of the living, and not of the dead' (*Luke* 20:38).

Solidarity as part of the living tradition of the church produces the development of popular organisation. Popular organisations renew the traditions of the church structures. In base Christian communities and in popular organisations such as the widows' group formed by Dolores or the women's group of Andrea in Usulután, the reading of the Bible goes together with the reading of the *realidad* of a country at war, and the conviction that God wants God's people to live a life where their human rights are respected. 'Human rights' becomes then a theological focus of reflection and a very important part of this living tradition of the church.

Theological method

The key theological category used by these women is 'memory'. Memory functions as the element which orders the hermeneutical circle of interpretation of the Scripture and also as the project for the future. Memory is used to relate to the past, to interpret life in the light of faith and past experiences; to the present, to make meaningful an existence with such a deep knowledge of suffering; and to the future, to think about the utopia of the reign of God in terms of what is known about the actions of God in their recent history. Lucía recalls how, in the flight from the Cuscatlán massacre many in the group 'saw God', that is, they knew God in a concrete way, as if God was also in the *guinda* with them. Memory, then, provides us with the following:

a) Memory gives women a community identity and religious identity. They remember who they are through key issues such as their gifts of organisation, courage and the obstinate faith which refused to accept the power of war as superior to God's power.

b) Memory provides women with concrete focuses of

reflection. One of these focuses is on women's bodies. Women are the ones who suffered their wombs being opened, as María Julia Hernández tells, and the cruelty of torture directed against their sexuality. Suyapa remembers how women fled to the mountains with their children. Lucía flees with her mother-in-law and her baby born two hours before the escape through the grass, without food or water. Violence hit the whole community, but women's bodies were hit even harder through hunger, torture focused on their sexuality and sufferings related to maternity. However, Doña Isabel reminds the community that after the war, 'women are raped even in their own homes', and now they organise themselves against domestic violence.

c) Memory, as a key for the simultaneous interpretation of the Bible and the *realidad*, produces an ethical reading of culture, religion and ideologies: In the same way that the writers of the Scriptures reflected theologically on their historical events, and discerned from them the ways of God in their life, the women of El Salvador identified issues of culture such as *machismo*, which they found un-Christian; they also criticised patriarchal church traditions. *Machismo* is a key element identified in their reflections, in relation to structures of power (ideology) and the construction of religious belief in Central America. Julia and her community read *Isaiah* 58 and *Hosea* 3 from that perspective.

2. The action-reflection-action circle
The main areas of the action-reflection-action circle are found in the development of a new spirituality, liturgy and community ethics.

Spirituality
The spirituality has been described by Nelly del Cid as 'nomadic'. Nelly considers it a spirituality on the move, not settled, with elements of expectation and discovery in this walk with God which is their theology. If the theology of liberation has been described as a *Caminata* (a walk), then

its spirituality should also be constantly moving forward. For Nelly, this is an essentially feminine walk because she sees the Holy Spirit as the feminine presence of God, constantly challenging the church and Christianity. Sister Patricia Farrell from Suchitoto also considers that we are now living the age of the Holy Spirit, which is essentially free, and gives us back the feminine face of God in a new way of being church in Central America. 'God came with these women', says Lucía in her theological remembrance of the action of the religious sisters during the war. The solidarity and courage of the sisters gave the people the concreteness of the presence of a living God among them. Moreover, this is the presence of the feminine face of God manifested through the faithfulness of religious women.

This spirituality is then reflected in a new ecclesiology, described by Mercedes as a non-hierarchical and democratic structure of the church. This new way to organise the church takes from the feminist movement a horizontal, participative nature, which is identified as the work of the Holy Spirit in our time.

Liturgy

The liturgy which accompanies this new ecclesiology has 'fewer words' and incorporates women's experience such as breastfeeding, as in the liturgies developed by Sister Patricia Farrell with her community. The courageous attitude of women during the war, challenging the 'principalities and powers' of the time, was inspired by a Jesus described as a 'big mouth' denouncing injustices and announcing the reign of God. The 'prophet' of the Hebrew scriptures has been described in popular terms as the rebel who refuses to shut up when confronting injustices. Interestingly, this also has liturgical consequences. Doña Isabel tells how fasting in the church has been incorporated as part of a living tradition of the church, and a liturgy for justice. The fasting she describes produced a transference of land that the community reclaimed, and also the formation of a committee to investigate murders committed. Since liturgy is the celebration of the presence of Christ among the people, praying and fasting now become part of the liturgical life of the persecuted, crucified church. However, the fasting and praying are not only done in the church. The *guinda* also includes a form of 'fasting' when whole communities fled without food, and sustained themselves by prayer and solidarity. The liturgy of the church has given way to the liturgy of life. The women share their ministry with their communities, celebrating life by refusing to accept death without resurrection.

Community ethics

Finally, the community ethics elaborated by these women concentrate on issues of violence, *machismo*, undemocratic structures in the church and in the government, and on family issues. *Machismo* is denounced as the main ideological root underlying domestic and state violence, and in the hierarchical, non-participative clerical and governmental organisations which obstruct the reconstruction of El Salvador after the war.

Family is an issue of increasing interest in Central American theology.[52] Families were divided during the war and, in some cases, a member of one's own family could become an enemy. Some women even left their families, losing their support during critical times when their vocation of solidarity for their people becomes a religious vocation too. Paradoxically, their religious community did not always become a family either. The family then seems to begin to be re-defined in what constitutes it. The vocation to join the people's struggle is a vocation of love for a family which exceeds the links of blood and membership of an organisation, because the links of compassion and the prophetic vocation to follow the 'big mouth' Jesus are stronger.

---

52. See, for instance, 'The Pastoral Challenge of the Latin American Family' in *Latin American Pastoral Issues*, CELEP, year XVIII, 1994.

The future of the theology of blossoming

This is the case where the past is the future. Sandra reflects on the subversive memory of the people as the key for a future dreamt by the women during the war. A future where women and men could work together in community, and solidarity would flourish against individualism, lack of hope and indifference. A future where hope will overcome the disillusionment produced by the fact that, after the war, so little seems to be gained in terms of the right to a dignified life and greater security for women who are still threatened by the ghost of old *machista* values, taken for granted before the war, but not any more. Nidia Díaz has said 'I don't want to go back to making *tortillas*', because the *tortillas* they made during the war were of a different kind. Those were *tortillas* of theological, political and cultural praxis for change. Their ingredients were courage, faith, strength in the organisation of the community and a critical awareness concerning the role of the church in Central America. They also gave as a gift to the world a way of doing 'real theology' (as Sister Peggy O'Neill called it, because liberation theology always has its starting point in reality) which may encourage women of other continents to do their own theology of blossoming, to go with them in their everyday lives and to transform Christianity in this, the *kairos* of women, and of poor women of Central America. A *kairos* where people see God 'coming with those women' who showed their obstinate solidarity during the war, and keep showing it afterwards, in the struggle to remain faithful to the example of Monseñor Romero and the multitude of anonymous saints of Central America. A *kairos* which is telling us that resurrection and theology are community issues and women's issues among the poor but wise women of El Salvador.

Bibliography

CAFOD/CIIR (1993) *Santo Domingo Conclusions*. London: CAFOD/CIIR.

CIIR (1980) *Reflections on Puebla*. London: CIIR.

CIIR (1992) *Step by Step Towards Peace in El Salvador. A chronology of the negotiations*. London: CIIR.

Freire, Paulo (1972) *Pedagogy of the Oppressed*. London: Penguin.

Galdámez, Pablo (1986) *Faith of a People. The life of a base Christian community in El Salvador*. London: CIIR.

Gutiérrez G, F McDonagh, C Padin OSB and J Sobrino SJ (1993) *Santo Domingo and After. The challenges for the Latin American church*. London: CIIR.

Hussey, Pamela (1989) *Free From Fear. Women in El Salvador's church*. London: CIIR.

López Vigil, María (1993) *Piezas para un Retrato* (Pieces for a Portrait). San Salvador: UCA Editores.

Macdonald, M and M Gatehouse (1995) *In the Mountains of Morazán. Portrait of a returned refugee community in El Salvador*. London: Latin America Bureau.

Mesters, Carlos (1989) *Defenseless Flower. A new reading of the Bible*. London: CIIR/Orbis.

Murphy, Claire Colette (1994) *An Introduction to Christian Feminism*. Dublin: Dominican Publications.

PAEM (Women's Educative Programme, Honduras) (1992) *La Mujer en la Iglesia y la Cultura Latinoamericana. Aporte de las Mujeres Latinoamericanas al la IV conferencia del Episcopado Latinoamericano* (Woman in the Church and in Latin American Culture. The contribution of Latin American women to the Fourth Latin American Bishops' Conference). PAEM.

'Pedro Arrupe' Jesuit Development Service (1994) *Tiempo de Recordar y Tiempo de Contar. Testimonios de comunidades repatriadas y reubicadas de El Salvador* (A time to remember and a time to tell. Testimonies by repatriated and relocated communities from El Salvador). San Salvador: 'Pedro Arrupe' Jesuit Development Service.

Ramos, Mario (undated) *Querido Guerrillero — Al año de la muerte de Camilo Turcios* (Dear Guerrilla — A year after the death of Camilo Turcios). El Salvador: (privately printed).

Romero, Oscar A (1985) *Voice of the Voiceless: The four pastoral letters and other statements of Archbishop Oscar Romero*. New York: Orbis Books, Maryknoll, 1985.

Romero, Oscar A (1993) *Archbishop Oscar Romero. A shepherd's diary*. London: CAFOD/CIIR.

Technofem SA de CV and PRODERE (1992) *Análisis de Género en Proyectos de Desarrollo* (Gender Analysis in Development Projects). El Salvador: Technofem SA de CV/PRODERE.

United Nations (1993) *De la Locura a la Esperanza, La Guerra de 12 Años en El Salvador* (From Madness to Hope, The 12-year war in El Salvador). Report of the Truth Commission for El Salvador. San Salvador/New York: United Nations.

Articles/journals

Ascencio, Isabel, 'Women Challenging the Revolution in Central America', *Challenge*, Vol 3, No 1, Spring 1992. Washington, EPICA.

Berryman, Phillip, 'The Coming of Age of Evangelical Protestantism', *LADOC*, November/December 1994.

Boff OSM, Clodovis, 'The Church in Latin America: Between perplexity and creativity', *SEDOS Bulletin*, 1995.

Del Cid, Carmen Manuela, 'El Salvador: Discovering a God who hides himself', *The Way*, January 1996.

Danner, Mark ,'The Massacre at El Mozote', *New Yorker*, 6 December 1993.

Kent, Judith, 'ARENA — A party for the people?', *Central America Report*, May/June 1994.

Mujeres por la Dignidad y la Vida, 'Hacer Política Desde las Mujeres' (Doing politics from a women's perspective). *Mujeres por la Dignidad y la Vida*, No 4, July 1993.

Ramírez, Isabel, 'Opening a Door to Women in El Salvador', *Challenge*, Vol 3, No 1, Spring 1992. Washington: EPICA.

Religious Task Force on Central America. *Central America Report*. Washington, December 1994.

Vigil, José María and Pedro Casaldáliga, 'Solidarity in Crisis: A reflection on the spiritual reality of solidarity in Latin America', *SEDOS Bulletin*, 1995.

About the authors

Marigold Best was until recently Latin American Programme Coordinator at Quaker Peace and Service. She has visited El Salvador and elsewhere in Latin America frequently and has written many articles for Quaker publications.

Sister Pamela Hussey has been with the Latin America section of CIIR since 1981. She has made many visits to Central America, principally El Salvador, and is author of the book *Free from Fear: Women in El Salvador's Church*, (CIIR 1989).

Founded in 1940, the **Catholic Institute for International Relations (CIIR)** has roots in the social justice tradition of the Catholic church. It is an independent charity which works for socially just development with people of any religious belief or none.

CIIR
Unit 3 Canonbury Yard
190a New North Road
London N1 7BJ
Tel: 44 (0)171 354 0883
Fax: 44 (0)171 359 0017

Incorporated with Limited Liability
Registered in England no.2002500
Registered office as above
Charity Registration no.294329